Take Control of Your Healthcare Costs

A GUIDE TO REDUCING YOUR MEDICAL EXPENSES IN THE AGE OF OBAMACARE

Barry Lionel Posner

Healthcare Publishers
Los Angeles, California

Copyright © 2014 by Barry Lionel Posner

All rights reserved. No part of this publication may be reproduced, distributed or transmitted in any form or by any means, including photocopying, recording, or other electronic or mechanical methods, without the prior written permission of the publisher, except in the case of brief quotations embodied in critical reviews and certain other noncommercial uses permitted by copyright law.

Take Control of Your Healthcare Costs / Barry Lionel Posner

Editor – Diane Cyr, Los Angeles, California
Book Layout © 2014 BookDesignTemplates.com
Author Photo – Suzannelandisphotography.com

ISBN-13: 978-1492296287
ISBN-10: 1492296287
Title ID: 4423757

Available from Amazon.com and other book stores

Printed in the United States of America by CreateSpace

Foreword

We all know healthcare costs are a serious problem, and most of us feel helpless to do anything about it. Even though the Patient Protection and Affordable Care Act (Obamacare) focuses on reducing costs and removing obstacles to healthcare, it goes only partway to making healthcare affordable to everyone.

The truth is, real cost containment isn't going to happen solely through the efforts of the government, or of hospitals or insurance companies. It has to happen because of consumer efforts. Each of us has a role in helping healthcare become more efficient, affordable and effective for everyone. This book provides a roadmap of how smart decisions can lead to instant cost savings.

Take Control of Your Healthcare Costs is a timely and personal guide to making financially savvy decisions. Author Barry Lionel Posner's knowledge of the healthcare system, and his experience in advising others about how to control medical costs, give readers insights and practical guidelines for bringing down their own expenses. Each chapter has practical tips and strategies for saving money without compromising care, as well as real-world examples of how people saved hundreds, even thousands, of dollars on their healthcare choices.

Readers will find this book filled with effective strategies for obtaining optimum value in the age of Obamacare.

Happy reading!

Preface

Thirty-five years ago, when he was just 41, my father died of leukemia. I was young, but still old enough to see how shaken my family was, not just physically and emotionally, but financially. As if the sickness and pain weren't bad enough, my parents (during the illness) had to cope with endless doctor visits, hospital stays, transfusions, chemotherapy and, of course, bills——piles and piles of bills.

Maybe it's no coincidence that healthcare financing became my passion. Over the years, what I've learned is this: While you can't control what happens to you, you can at least take one big worry off the plate—and that's how you're going to pay for it.

But here's something else I've learned: Hardly anyone has figured out how. Obamacare, Medicaid, Medicare, health savings plans, tax breaks, hundreds of insurance plans—who has time to sort through it all? If you're lucky and you've planned ahead, you may already have a great, high-value healthcare plan in place with trusted doctors and medical facilities at your beck and call. But, if you're like most folks I know, you'll start making your most important healthcare decisions at the moment when you're least capable of thinking clearly: When you're already in a crisis. And as my father used to say, you can't change the tires after you've already skidded off the road.

So that's why I decided to write this book. For 25 years, healthcare costs have been my business. After decades of negotiating contracts between healthcare providers and insurers, I've learned all the ways that consumers really can get the best care and the best coverage at the best cost. I know where the savings are, where mistakes are made, and where you can negotiate—that's right, bargain—for the best price. And I'm a very big advocate of making sure consumers know their healthcare options ahead of time, before disaster strikes.

For years, panicked family and friends have come to me with shopping bags filled with inscrutable paperwork and eye-popping invoices, asking for some way out of the mess. This book is for them, and for everyone else who has had only a dim view into the healthcare wilderness. I hope what light I can shed will put you on safe footing, physically and fiscally.

Here's to good health!

Acknowledgements

This book would not have happened without the sound advice of Bill Fordes and Michael Wallach, both of whom helped guide me in structure and content. Diane Cyr then took my words and concepts and masterfully edited them into this book, earning my eternal thanks for her clarity, organization and perseverance.

But my biggest thanks go to my family, who spontaneously supported me in my efforts through their encouragement, patience and understanding. To my wife Judy (always my moral compass), and my children, Jacob and Audrey: I am lucky to have your support, love and guidance.

Barry Lionel Posner

Contents

Chapter One: Playing the Insurance Game 19
   A Few Basics 19
   Today's Insurance Programs 21
   Read the Insurance Policy 30
   Where Obamacare Fits In 36

Chapter Two: Pick a Plan, Painlessly 39
   Fee-For-Service or Managed Care? 39
   How Much Coverage? 41
   What's It Going to Cost Me? 43
   Picking the Right Plan 46

Chapter Three: Government Assistance 53
   COBRA 53
   Community Assistance Programs 59
   Medicare – Are You Entitled? 64
   Medicaid to the Rescue 70

Chapter Four: Get Your Premium's Worth 75
   Read the Manual 76
   Make Sure You're Authorized 77

Timing Is Everything 79

Chapter Five: You Better Shop Around 85
How to Pick a Doctor 85

Doctor X vs. Doctor Y 87

Talk With Your Doc 88

In-Network vs. Out-of-Network 92

Concierge Medicine vs. Same Old 94

Chapter Six: Healthcare A La Carte 97
Retail Medical Clinic to the Rescue 98

Urgent Care Center vs. Emergency Room 100

Surgery Center vs. Hospital 102

Chapter Seven: Prescription Drug Options 107
Check Your Coverage 108

When Possible, Go Generic 109

Do Some Pharmacy Shopping 111

Chapter Eight: Handling Your Medical Bills 117
What's in Your Bill? 118

Learn to Spot Common Billing Errors 120

The Bill is Wrong—Now What? 122

Don't Wait—Negotiate 126

Chapter Nine: The IRS Can Be Your Friend 131

    Obamacare Premium Tax Credits 132

    Flexible Spending Account 132

    Health Savings Account 134

    Income Tax Deduction.................................. 135

    Retirement Account Hardship Distribution 136

Conclusion 139

Helpful Websites 143

Glossary 149

Index 157

To the Loves of My Life:

My Wife, Judy
My Son, Jacob
and
My Daughter, Audrey

"The First Wealth is Health."

—Ralph Waldo Emerson

Introduction

Healthy body, healthy wallet: Life is good when you've got both. Too often, though, it seems that one comes at the expense of the other. Even in the age of Obamacare, in which all United States citizens will be required to carry health insurance, one single healthcare crisis can be catastrophic. Even smaller, everyday healthcare decisions can nibble away at your cash and savings.

Why? For two reasons. One, healthcare costs keep going up, far faster than almost any other consumer expense. And two, many of us have no idea what to do about it. Sure, we all know how to accumulate airline miles, save 5 cents per gallon on gas, or find $2 sushi for lunch. But how many of us can answer the following questions:

- What do I do if my doctor is in-network but his anesthesiologist is not?
- If my 10-year-old son hurts his elbow skateboarding, should we go to the emergency room or urgent care?
- How much do I have to pay for new glasses if I lose my insurance?
- What if I get laid off and can't afford my Lipitor?

For most of us, looking at healthcare costs starts when we're already in a healthcare dilemma. And, like it or not, even the healthiest lifestyle has its financial healthcare pitfalls. Mammograms, colonoscopies, birth control, prostate exams—they're all necessary, and somebody's got to pay for them.

Use this book to sort through your options for choosing wisely and saving money. Chapter One gives a broad picture of the myriad healthcare options out there, including Medicaid, Medicare and, of course, Obamacare and the many private insurance choices. Chapter Two helps you decide which of those choices works best for you and your family. Following chapters help you find ways to save money on prescription drugs, surgeries, preventative care and even doctor visits. Finally, you'll learn how to "read" those Byzantine medical bills, find mistakes (80% of bills have them) and negotiate lower payments.

Whether you have a large family or none at all, whether you're self-employed or under-employed, chronically ill or doctor-avoidant, you can find the best health options at the best price. And you've already started by picking up this book.

<<>>

Chapter One: Playing the Insurance Game

A Few Basics

When you come right down to it, health insurance is really a form of gambling. By agreeing to pay the cost of your illness or injury, the insurance company is gambling you won't get sick. And, by agreeing to let the insurance company pay your doctor and hospital bills (in exchange for a monthly premium), you're gambling that you will.

That sounds like a lose/lose proposition, of course. Nobody *wants* hospital care, surgery, prescription drugs or even doctor visits. But as long as people get sick—and almost all of us do—insurance is a must. And, as a consumer, the only way to "win" the insurance game is to make sure you get the best healthcare coverage at the best cost.

The first step to winning is to understand the game. Start with these chapters. I'll break down what you need to know about how insurance works, how it's priced, what you get for your money and what you don't. Insurance is a gamble, and this is where you learn to stack the chips in your favor.

Insurance comes in many flavors, but all insurance *policies* (the contracts that outline your costs and benefits) share certain aspects:

- *None of them* covers everything.

- *All* require monthly payments (called *premiums*).

- *Most* limit coverage for certain chronic or pre-existing conditions.

- *Most* limit the amount of benefit paid out during the life of the policy. These *caps and maximums* can limit coverage for a certain illness, or for total healthcare costs over a certain period of time.

- *All* require certain other out-of-pocket expenses for consumers, including:
    - *Deductibles*: The amount of money you, the consumer, must pay for your healthcare expenses *before* your insurance covers certain costs.
    - *Copayments*: Relatively small charges you pay for each doctor visit and/or medical service.
    - *Co-insurance*: A percentage of the doctor/hospital bill you're required to pay, in addition to copayments and deductibles.

Today's Insurance Programs

Back in the day, if you had a job, you had health insurance. If you didn't have a job, you might have been on someone else's insurance—a spouse's or a parent's. Or if you were young and self-employed, you might have opted for "catastrophic" insurance—something that paid benefits only when you were likely seriously ill or injured. Or, you might have subscribed to that no-cost/no-benefit policy of crossing your fingers and hoping nothing happened.

These days, health insurance is no longer an all-or-nothing option. As you get older and gain dependents, you know you need at least some protection. And you also know that at least *some* of that cost burden will fall to you, even if you've got healthcare benefits from an employer, union or government program. That's because in this economy, nothing is a sure thing—not a job, not a benefit, not a union contract. You need to choose your care wisely because, ultimately, you're the one responsible.

Essentially, insurance comes in three categories: Group, government and individual. If you qualify for either a group or government program, you pay for only part (or possibly none) of your healthcare costs and premiums. But, if you require an individual program, you pay your premiums in full.

We'll get to government insurance programs in the next chapter. For now, if you're one of the millions who need and can pay (at least partly) for private insurance, start your shopping here.

Group Health Insurance – or Individual?

Group Health Insurance

If you're under 65 and employed, chances are you've got medical insurance through your union or employer. With group healthcare insurance, all members of your company or organization can pick among several coverage options for different monthly premiums. It's a good deal for insurers because, in gambling terms, group health insurance spreads the risk: The insurance company collects premiums from everyone, but pays out, for the most part, only to a few. It's also a good deal for the group because the larger the membership, the cheaper it is for everyone to "buy in." In short, employers like the low premiums; employees like getting healthcare benefits, and insurers like the guaranteed income - win/win/win.

Now here's the reality check. Group health insurance still has a cost, and these are cost-cutting times. Those employers that offer health insurance usually require employees to pay at least a portion of the premium.

So while group health insurance is still the best option for most working adults, it pays to closely investigate how much you'll be expected to pony up for the benefits you're offered. (More on that in the next chapter.)

> *Tip: To hold down the cost of group health insurance—for both you and your employer—join your company's wellness program. If your employer doesn't have one, lobby for one. Why? Simple math. Sick people cost money. Insurance companies negotiate corporate rates every year based on the previous year's payouts. The healthier the group, the lower the payouts. Companies may even pass on the savings by offering reduced premiums to wellness participants.*

Individual Health Insurance

As far as coverage goes, individual health insurance programs can look a lot like group healthcare programs. But as far as cost and eligibility goes, individual programs are a lot pricier and pickier. If you've got poor health, dependents, a dangerous job or advanced age—in other words, if you look like a bad risk—you're going to pay quite a bit for an individual healthcare plan.

> *Tip: If you're self-employed and private insurance is out of your budget, look into joining an organization or membership to take advantage of a group healthcare plan.*

Fee-For-Service vs. Managed Care

At times it seems there are as many insurance plans as there are magazines in a waiting room. So let's sort out the options.

FFS: Fee-for-service

How it works: Also called indemnity, fee-for-service (FFS) is your basic, traditional insurance plan, typically offered in employer-sponsored group health plans. You get basic coverage, including doctor visits, hospitalization and surgery. With a comprehensive FFS plan, you also get major medical, which pays the big bills for serious illness and injuries when basic coverage runs out. Plus you get to go to the doctor, clinic or hospital of your choice. The insurance company agrees to cover 80% of your medical bills after you meet your deductible each year, which can vary from $250 to thousands of dollars.

Pros:

- Versatility. You can go to any physician, or see a specialist without a referral.

- The healthier you are, the cheaper it is. If you've got a strong constitution and you're willing to risk your savings account, you can opt for a high deductible and pay a low monthly premium.

Cons:

- You have to know what's "reasonable and customary." If your doctor is out-of-network, and her fee is higher than what the FFS insurer considers reasonable and customary, you have to pony up the difference between the bill and what your insurer is willing to pay.

- Paperwork. It's up to you to submit bills for reimbursement.

Tonsil troubles: Gail's story

After a series of severe infections, Gail's six-year-old son had a tonsillectomy. Gail researched pediatric surgeons and found one in a nearby city with an excellent reputation. The surgery went smoothly, and the bill, which Gail paid with her credit card, was $1,600. Gail had already met her year's deductible, so she expected an 80% reimbursement, or $1,280. Instead, the insurance company stated that a "reasonable and customary" charge for a tonsillectomy was $1,200 and sent her a check for $960. Bottom line: Instead of laying out $320 for her son's procedure, Gail had to cover $620 of the bill. That included her expected 20% of the bill ($320) and the difference between the surgeon's charge and the insurance company's allowed amount ($300).

Managed-Care Program: HMO, POS and PPO

Generally more affordable than FFS programs, managed care insurance programs have three commonalities:

- *Focus on preventative health care*, such as wellness programs that emphasize exercise, nutrition and disease prevention.

- *Network contracts* with selected doctors, hospitals and other service providers. These providers offer reduced rates in exchange for the steady volume of managed-care patients.

- *Centralized billing and administrative functions*, which help keep down overhead costs and maintain affordable rates.

Bottom line: If you pick a managed-care program, you generally give up some freedom of choice, but gain some extra money in your wallet. You also start learning some fun new acronyms, since the three types of managed-care programs are HMO, PPO, and POS plans.

HMO: Health Maintenance Organization

How it works: When you belong to an HMO, you choose a primary care physician (PCP) within the network who then coordinates your medical care. Any time you need to see a specialist, the PCP must first refer you to one from within the network.

Pros:

- Cheaper than other managed-care plans.

- All "well" visits typically covered.

- No deductible—just a small co-pay per visit (usually $10-$25).

- Includes physicians, specialists, emergency care and hospitalization.

Cons:

- Limited choice of healthcare providers.

- Does not cover use of specialists or health services outside network.

- May cover only generic prescription drugs instead of brand-name.

- Does not pay for services not deemed medically necessary (i.e., cosmetic surgery).

POS: Point of Service Plan

How it works: By combining features of an HMO and FFS, the POS plans encourage, but do not require, using providers within the network. As with an HMO, you pay only a small co-pay—no deductible—to see a primary care physician or other network medical provider. But, if you decide to use a provider outside the network, you must pay a deductible, as well as a co-insurance payment of about 30%-40% of the bill.

Pros:

- More flexibility in choosing health providers.

- No financial penalty for staying within network for health care.

Cons:

- Outside-of-network healthcare can be costly.

- Paperwork: Out-of-network healthcare bills must be submitted for reimbursement.

PPO: Preferred Provider Organization

How it works: If you belong to a union, pay dues to a large organization or work for a large group of employers, chances are you have the option of a PPO plan. A Preferred Provider Organization is a group of doctors and hospitals that provide medical service only to a specific group or organization, such as the Writer's Guild for screenwriters. Like a POS, a PPO gives you some flexibility within the managed-care program: You can choose a doctor outside your network, but you must pay a deductible and cover about 20% of the bill yourself.

Pros:

- Flexibility in choosing health providers, at a less punitive cost than a POS.

- Cap on out-of-pocket expenses, which means the insurer pays 100% of your policy's benefits after you spend a certain amount on medical care.

Cons:

- Still required to submit out-of-network bills for reimbursement.

- Copayments and insurance premiums do not count toward out-of pocket expense cap.

HDHP: High Deductible Health Plan

These plans are self-explanatory: They feature relatively low premiums and high deductibles—about $1,250 for an individual and $2,500 for a family. Although HDHP plans force you to pay a big chunk of out-of-pocket costs for health services, the good news is that you can use a health savings account or health reimbursement arrangement (see Chapter 8) to pay those costs. Using these accounts can also lower your federal tax obligation.

CHIP: Catastrophic Health Insurance Plan

Because this plan has the highest deductible, it's largely a "safety net" plan in case of accident or serious illness. Generally, you won't find benefits for prescription drugs, screenings or other types of health services. Also, you'll still have to pay thousands of dollars out of pocket before full coverage kicks in.

In some cases, "marketplace" catastrophic plans do offer some benefits to certain applicants, such as people under 30 or those whose income qualifies them for a "hardship exemption." Those folks receive three annual primary care doctor visits and preventative services at no cost. They also receive other essential health benefits after meeting the deductible.

Health Plans: A Summary

Plan	Advantages	Tradeoffs
FFS	• Freedom of choice in doctors, specialists, hospitals	• Higher payments for care • Less coverage for preventative health services • Submit bills for reimbursement
PPO	• Some freedom in directing your own health care • Little paperwork • Generally, copayments but no deductibles	• Must use network providers
HMO	• Free preventative care services: checkups, immunizations, some screenings • Less costly than other plans • Little if any paperwork	• Must coordinate care through a primary care physician • Smaller network of healthcare providers • Referrals necessary to see specialists or obtain other health services
POS	• More freedom in choosing doctors and specialists than HMO • Less costly than FFS	• Some out-of-network services will not be covered • Higher co-insurance payments required for out-of-network doctors • Must file claims for reimbursement

Read the Insurance Policy

Healthy, smiling faces...testimonials about fabulous care...praise for doctors who take care of everything—that's what we're all used to seeing on those shiny insurance brochures. Each company is expert at making you believe you'll be getting top-notch coverage at bargain-basement prices.

Don't read the brochures. Read the policies. That's where you'll find the real story about what your premiums will buy.

Don't be surprised to find these common exclusions and limitations:

- Pre-existing conditions. Yes, Obamacare promises insurance to all, regardless of whether you've had cancer, major depression or fibromyalgia. Right now, though, folks with pre-existing conditions better read the fine print. If you've let your previous coverage lapse for two months, most health plans will make you wait six months to a year before paying out for your health condition.

> **No free lunch: Jack's story**
>
> *Jack, a diabetic who was otherwise in excellent health, left his retail job to follow his dream of working in community theater. Legally, he was entitled to extend his company's healthcare coverage through COBRA (described in the next Chapter), but he balked at paying the $352 monthly premium while he was without a steady income. Fortunately, Jack stayed in good health and got a managerial job at a small theater three months later. Unfortunately, his next insurer would not cover diabetes complications for six months. When Jack developed diabetes-related foot problems four months into his job, he was responsible for all medical bills - totaling $2,500 - all of which came out of Jack's pocket, and none of which applied to his annual deductible. The approximately $1,000 Jack would have paid in premiums on COBRA would have saved him at least that amount if he'd maintained health coverage.*

- Cosmetic surgery. If you have visible injuries from a car accident, or have a child with a birth defect, reconstructive surgery is almost always covered. But if you want an eyelid lift or nose job—and there's no medical need for it—it's likely to happen only on your own dime.

- Non-traditional treatments. Many folks swear by the health benefits of yoga, acupressure, massage and biofeedback. Most health plans, however, do not. Check your plan carefully if you wish to rely on so-called alternative medicine as part of your health treatment.

- Non-traditional drugs. Hair-growth stimulants, vitamins, homeopathic preparations—you're not likely to find any of them included in your healthcare plan.

- Home-care and private nursing care—these are often excluded by healthcare plans.

Pinpoint relief: Diane's story

Diagnosed with Stage 2 colon cancer at age 40, Diane followed her oncologist's orders to the letter—except when it came to relief from chemotherapy symptoms of aches and nausea. The prescribed drugs gave her stomach pain and little benefit, so she took a friend's suggestion and tried acupuncture. One session prior to each chemo treatment improved her appetite and energy level, which made the $75 payment well worth it. Moreover, because her oncologist had also recommended acupuncture, Diane's PPO paid 40% of the bill upon submission for reimbursement.

What are you (literally) waiting for?

Insurance plans and waiting periods are like love and marriage in the old Sinatra song: You can't have one without the other. Most plans designate specific waiting periods before kicking in some or all of your healthcare coverage. These include:

- Employer waiting period. New employees may have to wait three months or so before being eligible for healthcare benefits. This is usually to avoid a hit-and-run by employees who file a large claim right after joining—and then leave the company.

- Affiliation period. Typically, HMOs impose a waiting period of no more than three months before covering a new member.

- Pre-existing conditions exclusion period. If you've had a biopsy, medical treatment or diagnosis of a chronic medical condition within six months of applying for health insurance, you'll likely be sidelined from full coverage for one to 18 months (*see Jack's story, above*). *Exception*: You've had group health insurance coverage for at least a year prior to applying for the new plan, and you've gone two months or less between plans.

"Insurance? I'll take my chances."

If you're still convinced you can't afford a healthcare plan, stay tuned. Chances are you'll still qualify for a safety-net program, such as:

- Medicare, which covers disabled and senior Americans

- Medicaid, which covers low-income folks, or those ineligible for most types of private or group insurance

- Private organizations and nonprofits, which help applicants based on age, ethnicity, income, religious affiliation or type of illness

> ### *"I Don't Like My New Doctor!"*
>
> *Alice's problem: During the past six years of chronic migraines, Alice had been seeing Dr. Cheviot, a neurologist who specialized in headache pain management. Then Alice's HMO parted ways with Dr. Cheviot, and her PCP referred her to the network's other neurologist, Dr. Gastov. Dr. Gastov, however, changed Alice's medical care and drug protocol, which Alice claimed made her problem worse. Her options: See Dr. Cheviot out-of-network and pay $300 per visit or see Dr. Gastov and put up with more frequent pain.*
>
> ***Solution:*** *HMO members with pre-existing conditions are often eligible for "continuity of care" services. Because Alice had a longstanding medical condition being treated by an in-network doctor, she could continue seeing Dr. Cheviot at in-network copayment rates, even though he was no longer in her HMO. Exception: Continuity of care applies only with certain pre-existing*

conditions and situations. Call your health plan to see if you're eligible.

"This Isn't Reasonable and Customary!"

Jill's problem: Jill's son accidentally fell into a dining room window, ending up with a severe, but not life-threatening, cut on his arm. Hoping to minimize scarring and disfigurement, Jill took the child to a plastic surgeon, who spent an hour putting in 100 stitches. The bill was $3,500, which Jill submitted to her FFS healthcare plan. The insurer countered that a "reasonable and customary" treatment would have been 15 minutes of stitching at a cost of $300. The company sent her a check for $240, or 80% of the approved amount—which Jill did not consider anywhere near appropriate given the severity of her son's injury.

Solution: Health plans are regulated by state agencies, which means any number of state watchdogs can help Jill. For example, if Jill is a California resident, certain state groups can help her appeal a denied authorization. These include the following:

- For HMO disputes: California Department of Managed Healthcare (www.dmhc.ca.gov)

- For PPO disputes: California Department of Corporations (www.corp.ca.gov)

- For other insurance plans: California Department of Insurance (www.insurance.ca.gov)

- For physician disputes: Medical Board of California (www.californiamedlicense.com)

- For hospital disputes: California Department of Health Services (www.dhs.ca.gov)

> *Tip: Follow specific guidelines for filing complaints and disputes. Be prepared to submit a written appeal. With a strongly worded, clearly documented, written appeal, Jill has a shot at collecting more money from her insurer.*

Where Obamacare Fits In

Naturally, the Patient Protection and Affordable Care Act, signed into law by President Barack Obama, has an important role in both your healthcare and your health insurance needs. Controversy aside, the aim of Obamacare is to ensure that all citizens have access to basic, affordable health insurance. So, in a nutshell, here's how Obamacare affects you.

If you have insurance already, Obamacare gives you the following benefits:

- *Protection* against being denied insurance for pre-existing conditions

- *Coverage* for chronically ill children

- *Limiting* of copayments, deductibles and out-of-pocket maximums

- *Limiting* of premium increases without state approval

- *Mandatory coverage* of the following essential health benefits:
    - *Emergency services*
    - *Hospitalization*

- *Laboratory tests*
- *Maternity and newborn care*
- *Mental health and substance abuse treatment*
- *Dental and vision care for children*
- *Outpatient care*
- *Prescription drugs*

If you do not have or have not been able to afford insurance, Obamacare provides the following:

- *Ability to buy basic coverage at reasonable cost* through a state health insurance exchange

- *Tax credits*

- *Eligibility* for reduced copayments and deductibles

- *Ability to purchase coverage* regardless of pre-existing conditions

Moreover, under Obamacare, any citizen who does not buy health insurance will have to pay a penalty. In 2014, the penalty is $95 per person, or 1% of income, whichever results in a larger fine. By 2016 the penalty will increase to $695 or 2.5% of income.

In short, Obamacare does not change the quality of the care you are entitled to, nor does it create a government-run healthcare system. Its purpose is to reduce the number of uninsured Americans. It's still up to you to sort through which insurance plan works best for you, and at what price.

This is just a brief overview of some of the aspects of Obamacare that impact you directly. To learn about these in more detail - and to learn about additional aspects - below are three good websites:

- Obamacare Facts
  (www.Obamacare.com)
- Center for Medicare and Medicaid Services
  (www.healthcare.gov)
- U.S. Department of Health and Human Services
  (www.hhs.org)

<<>>

Chapter Two:
Pick a Plan, Painlessly

Now that you've walked around the showroom of healthcare insurance plans, it's time to ask the big question: Which plan is going to work best for you and your family? Like automobiles, major appliances and places to live, healthcare plans are big commitments, and rarely does the perfect one jump out at you. Some choices might make better sense for your wallet, and some might make better sense for your health situation, or for your risk tolerance, or even for your peace of mind.

> Tip: The better you know yourself and your needs—and, of course, the better informed you are of your choices—the happier you'll be with your health plan.

Fee-For-Service or Managed Care?

Whether you're deciding between plans offered by your employer, or whether you're contemplating an individual health plan, you need to know if you're the type who prefers the freedom of fee-for-service (FFS), or the lower cost of managed care. Ask yourself:

- *Are you proactive or reactive?* Do you get your oil changed regularly, check your fluid levels, and hit the gas station before the tank gets to one-quarter full? You're a proactive type, and you'd probably benefit from a managed-care plan that covers regular checkups and other preventative care. But, if you're the type who doesn't bring the car in until you smell burning metal, you might be more of a FFS customer.

> Tip: If you have children, or plan to, preventative care is a must. Make sure your plan covers the regular checkups essential to healthy pregnancies and childhoods.

- *Do you send your doctor holiday cards?* If your doctor is a treasured friend to your family, you probably want a FFS healthcare plan that covers visits to her office. But, if you can barely remember your doctor's first name, you might be happy with a lower-cost, managed-care program that operates with a network of doctors and hospitals.

> Tip: Before you decide against managed care, check the plan's provider directory. If your treasured doctor is part of a managed-care network, you may be quite happy to forego FFS.

- *Do you have more than 10 doctors on speed-dial?* If you make regular trips to a dermatologist, gastroenterologist, orthopedist, podiatrist or any other specialist, you'll find it tedious work to keep going back to a primary physician in order to get a referral. HMO managed-care programs require referrals to specialists; FFS does not.

> *Tip: Even if you follow the managed-care protocol, your PCP may not always give you a referral. If your doctor doesn't think you need a specialist, you'll have to pay for one out of pocket.*

How Much Coverage?

Before Obamacare, insurance companies could sell medical coverage a la carte: You could buy policies that didn't cover doctor visits, or prescription drugs, or maternity care.

Now, however, all policies must cover certain essentials, including medications and preventative care (see Chapter One for the full list). Moreover, all citizens must buy some kind of healthcare policy or pay a financial penalty for going without.

If you want more than just the "essential" coverage, you've got to pick a plan that goes beyond. Check your employer's Summary of Benefits and Coverage to see whether you can get the vision, dental or other healthcare coverage that's important to you. Or shop the marketplace for the plans that meet your requirements for total care. Just remember: The more benefits you require, the more you're likely to pay.

- *Ask: What happened last year?*

Past events are the best indicators of future events. If your daughter Susie needed braces, son Bobby broke his arm skateboarding, and spouse Isabel had a pre-cancerous mole removed, it's a pretty good bet that you'll need some coverage for orthodontia, emergency room visits and health screenings. Check your plans carefully for maximum annual limits of coverage and calculate your exposure for out-of-pocket expenses.

- *Ask: What are my "must-haves"*

If you're pregnant, or plan to be, you must have maternity care. If you have a history of cancer or heart disease, you must have screening and preventative care. And, if you have any other chronic condition, you must have access and coverage for appropriate care. Compare your "must-have" list with your plan's Summary of Benefits. Remember: When it comes to your health, there's no free ride. If you choose not to pay for coverage, you will likely pay for the medical care itself.

- *Ask: What if...?*

As in: What if I need help for anxiety or depression? What if this insomnia is a symptom of something more serious? What if I get that bad flu that's going around? You may not need help for any of these things, but, if something's niggling at you, having coverage will give you peace of mind.

> *Tip: Prescription drugs, far and away, are likely to be your biggest health expense, particularly as you get older. Make sure you look carefully through your plan's formulary to learn which medications will be covered in the event you need them.*

What's It Going to Cost Me?

Like fingerprints and snowflakes, it seems that no two insurance plans are alike—at least when it comes to calculating how much you'll have to pay for coverage. Most insurance plans require four types of payments (premiums, co-pays, deductibles and co-insurance), and those are applied to dozens, even hundreds, of different types of benefits. To compare co-pays and co-insurance requirements for, say, six different healthcare plans with 10 different premium and deductible levels would make even a statistician throw down his pencil.

So here's a quick review of what you need to know. (Remember the details back in Chapter One?)

Generally, all plans require these payments:

- *Premium:* The amount you pay each month to maintain coverage.

- *Copayment:* The amount paid each time you see a doctor, receive a healthcare service or purchase prescription drugs.

- *Deductible*: The amount you pay out-of-pocket before the insurance company begins paying for your medical claims.

- *Co-insurance*: The amount you pay for covered medical services after you've paid your copayment or deductible. (For instance, after you've met your deductible, your insurance company pays 80% of the cost of your knee replacement; you pay the co-insurance of 20%.)

Moreover, all plans have the following:

- *Maximums and caps*: These are the total out-of-pocket costs (except co-pays and premiums) you are obliged to pay for medical expenses during a year. After you've reached a designated "maximum"—say, $5,000—your insurance company covers all other medical expenses for the year. (Obamacare has set out-of-pocket maximums for 2014 at $6,350 for an individual and $12,700 for a family—but you can find plans with lower limits.)

Finally, most people believe this number is the most important to consider when choosing a healthcare plan:

- *The premium.*

Most people are wrong. The most important cost consideration is what we'll discuss next.

Avoiding deductible trouble

Simple math: The higher the deductible, the lower the premium. That's the way it works for any insurance, whether auto, homeowner, or healthcare. And that's why most people who want to save money now will opt for a high deductible and low monthly premium.

But in health insurance it's really not so simple. Here are a few examples:

The $4,800 headache: Maria's story

Maria, a 30-year-old accountant, was shopping with her 15-month-old son when she suddenly passed out. The clerk called an ambulance, which rushed her to a nearby emergency room. Although doctors could not determine why she lost consciousness, the cost for the diagnostic tests and ambulance came to $5,800. Maria's group health plan had a $5,600 annual deductible, of which she and her husband had already paid $800. They now had to pay $4,800 out of pocket, and needed to work out a six-month payment plan with the hospital to do so.

"I just won't get sick": Barbara's story

Barbara, a 42-year-old receptionist, had a hard time finding an insurance plan that would fit her modest budget. Finally, she opted for a plan that cost just $123 per month and had a $3,300 deductible. Because Barbara has very little in savings or disposable income, she simply does whatever she can to avoid seeing a doctor, and crosses her fingers against having an accident or serious illness.

Picking the Right Plan

In a nutshell, here's what's important to consider when picking the deductible (and the premium) that's best for you.

Pick a plan with a lower deductible if:

- *You have pre-existing health conditions*

The more medical care you require throughout the year, the more likely it is you'll reach your deductible quickly and have coverage for your healthcare expenses.

- *You don't have substantial cash reserves*

Don't gamble your emergency funds on medical needs. And, if you don't have an emergency fund, you'll find it very expensive to finance unanticipated hospital stays, surgeries or illnesses.

- *You are middle-aged or older*

Age itself is a medical risk. The older you are, the more likely you'll be tackling health problems, so the more likely you'll use up your deductible.

- *You have a family*

You and your spouse and kids may all be young and healthy, but, if you're all injured in an accident, the cost of care could be astronomical. Make sure you're financially ready for any "what-ifs."

- *You just like peace of mind*

Many who can afford a high deductible simply prefer a lower one. They'd rather pay the higher premium and know they'll be covered if something goes wrong.

Pick a plan with a higher deductible if:

- *You are single, young and healthy*

Congratulations! You're not likely to require thousands of dollars worth of medical care. If you do, you'll be able to work out the financing without jeopardizing your kids' college funds.

- *You're a strong money manager*

Say a $250 monthly premium comes with a $4,000 deductible, and a $450 premium comes with a $2,000 deductible. If you choose the higher deductible and lower premium—and you don't require much health care—you can put aside the extra $200 per month and save the amount of the difference in deductibles in just 10 months. That gives you a good cushion to meet future healthcare costs without paying a higher premium.

- *You can tap your cash reserves*

When you pay a premium, you are essentially letting the insurance company take control of your money in the event it's needed for medical care. Therefore, many people who can afford it prefer to keep that money—as much as possible—in their own accounts. For them, it's worth it to pay for medical care out of pocket and let the insurance company take over only when necessary.

And remember: Deductibles are not caps!

Even after you've paid your deductible, you still must pay certain medical expenses. These include premiums, copayments and co-insurance. So keep that in mind as well when picking the deductible you can afford.

More money saving tips:

- *The more frequent your doctor visits*, the *lower* your copayment should be. If you have children or take medications often, those copayments can add up. But if you can't remember your last doctor visit or trip to the pharmacy, a higher copayment is a lot easier to tolerate—and often comes with a lower premium.

- *High deductibles and low incomes don't add up*. You might think you're saving money with a high deductible and low premiums, but unexpected costs can make life miserable if you don't have the coverage.

> Tip: Keep your deductible to no more than 5% of your gross annual income.

- *Accidents happen, even to health eaters and marathon runners.* Generally, the healthier you are, the more risk you can tolerate in your healthcare plan. But one hospital stay can cost tens of thousands of dollars, so if you choose a high-deductible plan make sure your savings can cover the "what ifs."

- *Don't overbuy.* If you live in a $100,000 house, you don't drive a Bentley. So don't get a Cadillac insurance policy if your budget is more in the Ford Focus category. If you're young and healthy, it's okay to take the risk of a high deductible and pay lower out-of-pocket costs per month.

- *Know the limits of coverage.* Even though Obamacare eliminated coverage limits on such "essentials" as maternity care, insurance companies can still impose limits on certain nonessential medical services. Check your plan for coverage limits on screenings, MRIs, physical therapy and other medical care.

- *Factor in your dependents.* If you have adult kids 26 or younger, they can now remain on your policy if they have no coverage through an employer. Moreover, policies cannot exclude coverage for kids under age 19 who have pre-existing health conditions.

- *Compare and contrast.* It takes only a few minutes to review the main benefits of a healthcare plan, so don't pick the first one that comes along. What looks appealing at first glance—low premiums, lots of coverage—might end up costing you in high co-payments, deductibles and co-insurance obligations.

- *Finally, know when you need more care than you can possibly afford.* If you're over 65, disabled, low-income or otherwise unable to afford health insurance, you may qualify for Medicare or Medicaid. See Chapter Three for more details.

The Obamacare Packages

Individuals and small groups are now eligible for Obamacare plans, which offer various combinations of premiums, copayments and co-insurance. Each plan must cover the "essentials" (listed in Chapter One), and each is priced by standardized "tiers."

- *Bronze* plans have the lowest monthly premiums and cover about 60% of the average member's total healthcare costs.

- *Silver* plans, with higher premiums, cover 70% of healthcare costs.

- *Gold* plans cover 80% of healthcare costs.

- *Platinum* plans, which have the highest premiums, will cover 90% of healthcare costs.

Keep in mind that all Obamacare plans cover the essentials and that tax credits and other financial aid is available based on income.

In Summary: The Least You Need To Know

- Know your personality tolerance for risk

- Make a list of must-haves

- Focus on the deductible, not the premium

- Don't overbuy—keep deductibles to less than

- 5% of gross annual income

<<>>

Chapter Three: Government Assistance

Our government provides many forms of healthcare assistance, mainly COBRA, community assistance programs, Medicare and Medicaid. Here are some strategies, then, for making the most of government healthcare programs.

COBRA

For many workers, losing a job doesn't just mean losing an income. It means losing health benefits. Fortunately, if you were part of a group health plan in a company with more than 20 employees, federal law says you're entitled to receive continuing coverage under COBRA—the Consolidated Omnibus Budget Reconciliation Act, passed in 1986. Unfortunately, COBRA can come with a pretty hefty price tag. And, if you're already wondering how you're going to pay your bills, COBRA can seem like an extravagance.

So let's take a look at what's really at stake when you're faced with the COBRA choice. Do you join up, opt out, or look for some other health option?

What you get

- *The same coverage you're used to.* With COBRA, you receive exactly the same healthcare benefits you received on the job, and so do your dependents. Certain "qualifying events" can trigger up to 36 months of COBRA coverage, but in the case of most job losses, you and your family are entitled to 18 months of benefits.

- *Health insurance portability.* If you drop your healthcare coverage for more than 63 days, you risk having any pre-existing conditions excluded from future healthcare plans. COBRA gives you continuity of coverage, which protects your "health insurance portability." In other words, if you had a cervical biopsy during your employment, and then opt out of COBRA because you're currently healthy, your next group healthcare plan may limit coverage on reproductive disorders. But, if you *don't* show a large gap in coverage, your next healthcare plan *must* offer coverage, regardless of past medical history.

- *Open enrollment rights.* If you're on COBRA, you're entitled to the same enrollment opportunities as active employees. So when your former employer offers open enrollment, you can switch health insurance plans if you choose.

- *Retroactive benefits.* You have 60 days to decide whether you want COBRA or not. If on Day 59 you're diagnosed with diabetes, you'd still be covered from the moment you lost your previous healthcare plan, provided you pay the retroactive premiums. Moreover, your medical bills incurred during that period would be covered as well.

What it costs

The cost varies by employer, but generally COBRA costs 102% of your monthly total health insurance premium (including the employer portion). In other words, if your group health premium was $450 per month, but your employer paid $320 as an employment benefit, you'd have to pick up the full monthly tab, plus a 2% administrative fee. You'd also have to pick up any deductibles, copayments or other benefits your employer may have paid. So instead of paying $130 out-of-pocket for your healthcare every month, you'd pay $450, plus $9 (the 2% fee), plus, say, another $500 or so in annual deductibles and other costs.

> *Tip: Certain COBRA participants can receive up to a 65% federal subsidy for up to 15 months. Talk to your employer or contact the Department of Labor (www.dol.gov) for more information.*

How you qualify

- *You lose your job* through layoff, retirement, quitting, being fired (except if you break the law, etc.) or working too few hours to qualify for benefits.

- *Your employer has 20 or more employees.* In some states, workers in companies with 2 to 19 employees may also be eligible to continue their group health plans under state "mini-COBRA" laws.

- *You are a dependent* of a qualified COBRA recipient. Spouses and children are entitled to 36 months of coverage in the event of divorce (or legal separation), death, or eligibility for Medicare. Also, spouses, dependent children and children who lose their dependent status under their parent's plan can sign up for COBRA independently. In other words, if your child becomes sick within 60 days of the job loss, he or she can still get coverage without your signing up for COBRA.

Is it worth it?

YES, if:

- *You do not find comparable private individual health insurance rates.* (Remember: You have 60 days to look around!).

- *You have pre-existing conditions and need continuity of coverage.*

- *You value peace of mind.* COBRA may not be cheap, but it's less expensive than an accident, serious illness or pregnancy—all of which can happen whether you're employed or not.

NO, if:

- *You have definite plans to move or look for work elsewhere in the country.* Generally, health plans want you to use their local provider network. If you live in New York and you're job-hunting in Texas, COBRA will not cover you unless you fly back to New York for medical care.

- *You're healthy, single and likely to find a less-expensive healthcare alternative.* If you weigh the cost of premiums against the expected cost of medical services, you might well find that you can live comfortably with lower premiums and fewer benefits than those offered by COBRA.

- *Your employer is not legally obligated to offer COBRA. For instance:*
    - The company goes out of business. (Exception: Retirees can file for COBRA if their former employer files for bankruptcy.)
    - The company drops its group healthcare coverage completely.
    - The company's size drops to less than 20 employees.

Clearly, the COBRA question is hardly clear-cut. As with many insurance plans, COBRA's upside—good healthcare benefits—is pitted against the downside of its cost. If you are accustomed to paying only a fraction of your healthcare premiums, the price of COBRA can be a real slap to the wallet.

But here's the good news: You've got 60 days to think about it. So use that time researching other insurance options, weighing costs and benefits, and, of course, job hunting. If you need COBRA, it will be there for you, and may well be worth the price of the premiums—even the retroactive ones.

In Summary: The Least You Need to Know

- COBRA extends your health benefits for a minimum of 18 months if you lose your job.

- You have 60 days to decide whether to continue your coverage on COBRA.

- COBRA must be offered by companies with a group plan and more than 20 employees.

- COBRA costs 102% of the full employee premium charged by the insurance company.

- COBRA is critical for healthcare "portability" (ensuring that your next insurance plan will accept you, despite any pre-existing conditions).

- COBRA is less critical for single, healthy adults, more critical for families and those with ongoing health issues.

Community Assistance Programs

Free and low-cost medical care is as close as your local community—and you don't have to be low-income to get help. After all, one cancer diagnosis can cost from $7,000 to $30,000 to treat; a chronic illness, such as multiple sclerosis, can require hundreds of thousands of dollars' worth of medication over a lifetime. If you need more help than you can afford, there's a community assistance program that can get you what you need.

Here's where you can get started.

To locate clinics in your area:

- National Association of Free Clinics (www.freeclinics.us) has connections with more than 1,200 low-cost or free clinics.

- Care Harbor (www.careharbor.org) works with local medical communities to organize medical clinics to provide quality free medical services.

- Planned Parenthood (www.plannedparenthood.org) offers limited screenings, exams, vaccines, and family planning services.

- The HealthWell Foundation (www.healthwellfoundation.org) offers medical-payment assistance for qualified applicants.

- The Department of Health and Human Services (www.hhs.gov) has information on medical financial assistance for low-income families.

For general cancer-related illnesses:

- National Cancer Institute (www.cancer.gov)
- American Cancer Society (www.cancer.org)
- Cancer Financial Assistance Coalition (www.cancerfac.org)
- CancerCare (www.cancercare.org)
- The Cancer Support Community (www.cancersupportcommunity.org)
- Association Cancer On-line Resources (www.acor.org)

For breast cancer:

- American Breast Cancer Foundation (www.abcf.org)
- Avon Foundation (www.avonbreastcare.org)
- Susan G. Komen Foundation (www.komen.org)
- BreastCancer.org (www.breastcancer.org)
- Advanced Breast Cancer Community (www.advancedbreastcancercommunity.org)

For prostate cancer:

- Prostate Cancer Foundation (www.pcf.org)
- Prostate Cancer Info Link (www.prostatecancerinfolink.net)
- Zero: The Project to End Prostate Cancer (www.zerocancer.org)
- Us TOO (www.ustoo.com)
- Prostate Conditions Education Council (www.prostateconditions.org)

For diabetes:

- American Diabetes Association (www.diabetes.org/in-my-community/programs)
- Diabeteslocal (www.diabeteslocal.org)
- American Association of Diabetes Educators (www.diabetesselfcare.org)
- National Diabetes Information Clearinghouse (www.diabetes.niddk.nih.gov)
- Charles Ray III Diabetes Association, Inc. (www.cr3.org)

For heart disease:

- American Heart Association (www.heart.org and www.hearthub.org)
- Cleveland Clinic Heart Center (www.clevelandclinic.org/heartcenter)
- American College of Cardiology (www.acc.org)
- Mended Hearts, Inc. (for heart surgery patients) (www.mendedhearts.org)

- Heart Rhythm Society (www.hrsonline.org)

For stroke:

- National Stroke Association (www.stroke.org)
- American Stroke Association (www.strokeassociation.org)
- The Internet Stroke Center (www.strokecenter.org)
- RTH Foundation (www.rthfoundation.org)
- The Stroke Network (www.strokenetwork.net)

For clinical trials:

- The U.S. National Institutes of Health provides information to those who want to participate in clinical studies of various illnesses. ClinicalTrials.gov (www.clinicaltrials.gov) currently lists more than 150,000 studies with locations in all 50 states and in 185 countries.

For rare, serious and/or chronic illnesses:

- The National Organization of Rare Disorders (www.rarediseases.org) can guide you to specific organizations that provide resources for specific illnesses.

- Patient Advocacy Foundation (www.patientadvocate.org) provides financial assistance for those with chronic and serious conditions.

- Survivorship A-Z (www.survivorshipatoz.org) has resources and information for those with cancer and HIV/AIDS, including financial and living assistance.

- Patient Access Network Foundation (www.panfoundation.org) offers access to breakthrough medical treatments for those with certain chronic and life-threatening diseases.

- Advocacy for Patients with Chronic Illness, Inc. (www.advocacyforpatients.org) provides a wide range of financial, legal, and insurance-related services for those with chronic illnesses.

The community to the rescue:

For three years, Marc has been unemployed and without health insurance and was recently diagnosed with type 2 diabetes. Although he is trying his best to improve his health, he has gone through his savings and is worried about affording his medications.

After some online research, Marc found two patient assistance organizations that could help. He got a free diabetes care kit from Xubex that included a blood glucose meter, lancet device, carrying case and test strips. He also got substantial discounts for an insulin pump and pump supplies from the Charles Ray III Diabetes Association. Marc now receives diabetes medications worth hundreds of dollars per month, and checks in with a local free clinic while he looks for work.

In Summary: The Least You Need to Know

- You don't have to be broke to get assistance—just sick!

- The Internet is your best friend when you need help.

- Nearly every chronic illness has an organization designed to help with treatment plans and resources.

- Don't forget that clinical trials and experimental programs can be part of your healthcare protocol.

Medicare – Are You Entitled?

Our founding fathers never mentioned it, but at this point in our country's history Medicare is practically a constitutional right. If you're over 65 and a citizen, you likely qualify for Medicare—and so does your spouse, divorced spouse, widow or widower, or dependent parent.

Because you've earned it, Medicare is an entitlement program—not needs-based—and its rules are the same regardless of where you live. Here's the nutshell version.

Who's entitled?

- 65 years old *and*

- US citizen or legal resident for five consecutive years, *and*
- Contributor to Social Security taxes for at least 10 years, *or*
- Spouse, ex-spouse, widow, widower or dependent parent of qualified Social Security wage-earner, *or*
- Under 65 and disabled, or with kidney failure

The A, B, C and D's of Medicare

You usually hear Medicare referred to by its "parts": hospital, medical, managed care and prescription drugs. Each has different eligibility requirements, rules and, in some cases, premium costs. These include:

Part A: Hospital

What it covers: Stays at hospitals and nursing facilities, and home health care.

What it costs: Nothing, if you or your spouse paid Medicare taxes while working.

Part B: Medical

What it covers: Most basic doctor and lab costs, some outpatient services (such as X-rays), medical equipment and supplies, and physical therapy.

What it costs: Because it's a voluntary program, members must pay an annual deductible ($147 in 2013) and monthly premium ($104.90). Premiums can vary based on income, and Medicare covers only 80% of approved costs.

What A and B don't cover:

- Long-term care
- Routine dental and vision care
- Dentures
- Cosmetic surgery
- Acupuncture
- Hearing aids and exams for fitting

Part C: Medicare Advantage

For Medicare recipients who want to customize their healthcare, Medicare Advantage combines Parts A and B into a managed-care package administered by an HMO or PPO plan. Private insurance companies provide some of the coverage, and details vary by individual. It's the most cost-effective option for you.

Part D: Prescription Drugs

What it covers: Varies by plan. To get Medicare prescription drug coverage, you must first join a plan run by an insurance company approved by Medicare. Prescription drug coverage can also be offered as part of your (Part C) Medicare Advantage Plan.

What it costs: Varies by plan and by income, but you must pay some monthly premium (between about $12 and $67 in 2013) in addition to your Part B premium. Once you've reached a certain out-of-pocket maximum, you automatically get "catastrophic coverage," which means you pay just a small co-insurance or co-pay amount for your prescription drugs.

Obamacare and prescription drugs for seniors

Those who have Medicare prescription drug coverage (Medicare Part D,) which pays for some but not all the costs of prescription drugs, often experience a coverage gap (i.e., a temporary limit on what the drug plan will cover for drugs). If you have Medicare Part D and you have a gap in coverage, you'll only have to pay 47.5% of the cost for covered brand-name prescription drugs. And what you pay for generic drugs during the coverage gap will decrease each year until it reaches 25% in 2020.

> *Tip: Once you qualify for Medicare, sign up for prescription drug coverage. Even if you don't have expensive prescriptions at the moment, chances are that you will at some point. If you wait until then, you'll have to pay a penalty for late enrollment.*

Still too expensive?

Clearly, Medicare doesn't mean seniors get a free ride after 65. You can't get prescription drugs, lab tests or even routine doctor visits without paying premiums. And you can't get routine vision care, hearing aids or alternative therapies at all. If you have Part A Medicare and a limited monthly income and savings, you might qualify for Medicare Savings Programs. Check out the following resources:

- Qualified Medicare Beneficiary Program (QMB): *Helps cover premiums, deductibles, co-*

insurance and copayments for Part A and/or Part B Medicare.

- Specified Low-Income Medicare Beneficiary Program (SLMB): *Helps pay Part B premiums only.*

- Qualified Individual Program: *Helps pay Part B premiums only; requires annual qualification.*

- Qualified Disabled and Working Individuals Program (QDWI): *Helps pay Part A premiums only. Working, disabled adults may qualify.*

And then there's Extra Help

Let's face it: Prescription drug costs, far and away, are the biggest headache for seniors and others who qualify for Medicare. *Extra Help* is a Medicare program designed to help cover your Part D expenses if you have limited income and resources. To see if you qualify:

- Visit www.socialsecurity.gov/i1020. Call Social Security at 1-800-772-1213

- Contact your State Medical Assistance (Medicaid) office at www.medicare.gov/contacts

- Contact your State Health Insurance Assistance Program

Medicare and private insurance: Who pays what?

The one constant in Medicare coverage is that...it isn't constant. Every year, your medical and prescription drug plan is likely to change, so make sure you stay informed. If you're worried that the drugs you're taking this year won't be covered next year, or that you can't keep seeing the doctor you've gone to for 10 years, do two things:

- Review your plan materials annually, and make sure your current plan will meet your needs for the following year.

- Look into secondary insurance, and then know who's going to pay what, and when.

Late to the party: Bill's story

After he turned 65, Bill knew he was entitled to Medicare, but decided to stay on his current insurance at his corporation, where he was still employed as a mid-level manager. He developed a severe bronchial infection and had several series of X-rays taken of his lungs. After he recovered, he submitted an $850 radiology bill to his company's FFS plan, expecting an 80% reimbursement. Instead, the insurer rejected the bill. Reason? In the insurer's view, anyone entitled to Medicare needs to enroll in Medicare—and Medicare must be the primary payer for any claims. The employer's insurance would then be the secondary payor, stepping in only after Medicare covered its part of the bill.

When Medicare is involved, it can be a hassle—to say the least—figuring out which insurer is going to cover which cost. In some cases, as in Bill's, Medicare Part B would be the primary payer. In other cases, the primary insurer might be a private company, with Medicare paying only those costs not covered by the primary insurer.

So here are some general guidelines in untangling the payment web:

- Accidents, worker's compensation and liability claims will almost always involve Medicare as a *secondary* payer.

- Healthcare providers, hospitals and pharmacies need to be informed of *all* your insurance plans.

- Doctors and healthcare providers who do *not* accept Medicare will likely cost you more.

- Your State Medical Assistance office (www.medicare.gov/contacts) and State Health Insurance Assistance Program (SHIP) can answer your questions about coverage and costs.

Medicaid to the Rescue

Unlike Medicare, Medicaid is a needs-based program, giving healthcare assistance to low-income families and individuals. Although it's a federal program, each state has its own rules and regulations about who qualifies and for which services. By and large, though, you qualify for Medicaid under these conditions:

- You meet the requirements of the Aid to Families with Dependent Children program.

- You are pregnant or are a small child in a family whose income is at least 133% below the Federal Poverty Level (FPL).

- You receive Supplemental Social Security.

- You receive adoption or foster care assistance.

- You are under age 19 living in a family at or below the FPL.

- You are a Medicare beneficiary in financial need.

Depending on the state, you can also receive Medicaid if you are low-income and disabled, "medically needy," or uninsured and screened for certain cancers or tuberculosis.

What it covers: Benefits can vary from state to state as well. But if you're on Medicaid, it's required that you receive the following:

- In-patient and out-patient hospital care
- Prenatal care
- Vaccines for children
- Physician services, including pediatric, nurse/midwife and nurse practitioner
- Nursing facility services
- Family planning services

- Home health care
- Lab and X-ray services
- Ambulance services
- Early and periodic screening, diagnostic and treatment for children
- Medicare deductibles and premiums

What it costs: Nothing, for emergency services or family planning services, or for pregnant women, minor children or qualified nursing home patients. Otherwise, states may impose nominal deductibles, co-insurance or copayments for certain recipients and services.

More resources:

- Supplemental Security Income (SSI) benefits. For financially struggling adults who are disabled, blind, or over age 65, the Social Security Administration provides cash benefits (not Social Security benefits) for help with food, clothing and shelter. (www.socialsecurity.gov).

- Children's Health Insurance Program (CHIP). For children in families that do not qualify for Medicaid—but can't afford private insurance—CHIP offers low-cost health insurance coverage. (www.insurekidsnow.gov).

The Obamacare Medicaid Reform

In the past, applying for Medicaid meant you needed to meet certain criteria, such as being pregnant, having a child or having a disability—and usually meeting an income requirement. With Obamacare the only main requirement is that you make less than 133% of the Federal Poverty Level. To find out if you are eligible for Medicaid, fill out an application at your state's health insurance marketplace. The application process will notify you if you are eligible for Medicaid.

Obamacare also improves access and quality to Medicaid services. Doctor payouts have been historically low, and, as a result, many doctors didn't take Medicaid and the quality of care tended to be poor. Obamacare Medicaid reform includes raising the amount doctors get paid to the same level of Medicare. It also increases payments to Medicaid programs that offer preventive services for free or at little cost. New free preventive services include tests for high blood pressure, diabetes, and high cholesterol; many cancer screenings, including colonoscopies and mammograms; counseling to help people lose weight, quit smoking or reduce alcohol use; routine vaccinations; flu and pneumonia shots; and other services.

In Summary: The Least You Need to Know

Here's the bottom line: At first glance, government healthcare programs seem to have more twists than a bowl of spaghetti. They're confusing, rule-saturated, and at times seemingly arbitrary.

But they help. The aim of Medicare, Medicaid and Obamacare is to ensure that nobody goes without healthcare coverage, regardless of age, income, employment or disability. When you get to know the rules of the government-run insurance game, you definitely have an edge on a better, more prosperous and healthier future, wherever your health and life might be at present.

Medicare:

- Entitlement-based
- For older and disabled citizens
- Can be combined with secondary insurance

	Coverage	Cost	Limitations
Part A	Hospitals, nursing care	Zero	Long-term care, vision, dental, hearing aids
Part B	Doctors, out-patient	Deductible and premium	Same as Part A
Part C	Managed care package	Varies	Same as Part A
Part D	Prescription drugs	Varies	Coverage gap

Medicaid:

- Needs based
- Lower-income and disabled citizens
- Covers basic health benefits
- Low and no cost, depending on eligibility

<<>>

Chapter Four: Get Your Premium's Worth

Like many folks her age, my grandmother owned a car she almost never drove. It was cleaned frequently, serviced regularly and given a prime space in her senior residence parking lot. When it rained, she worried it would rust; when it snowed, she fretted until a space was shoveled around it. "Just in case I need to get out," she would say.

Clearly, Grandma was not getting the best use out of her car. For the rest of us, a car is an everyday convenience; for her, it was a $10,000 security blanket. And I bring this up because that's exactly how many of us treat another major investment: our health insurance. Used thoughtfully, a healthcare policy can be an everyday convenience that truly helps us live better. Or it can be something we're afraid to "touch" unless it's an unavoidable emergency. Either way, a healthcare policy is something that costs most of us a fairly significant chunk of change, so why keep it parked on a shelf? In this chapter, you'll learn some smart ways to make the most of what you pay for. Stop enshrining your healthcare plan and start using it.

Read the Manual

Here is a conversation I had with my good friend the other day:

He: "I don't understand my healthcare benefits."
Me: "Have you reviewed your Evidence of Coverage?"
He: "What?"
Me: "The booklet you received with your policy that explains benefits and coverage."
He: "Who reads that stuff?"

When our office was first computerized 30 years ago, the tech guys were pestered daily with questions like, "How do you turn it on?" "How do you save this file?" "How do I print something out?" Their standard response was "RTM"—read the manual. Same with insurance policies. The EOC—Evidence of Coverage—lists everything that's covered (your benefits) and everything that's not. If you review it just a few times a year, you'll automatically know the answers to such questions as:

- "How many sessions are covered for psychological therapy?"

- "Can I get a private room at the hospital?"

- "What percentage do I have to pay for X-rays?"

- "Am I covered for genetic cancer testing?"

The truth is, when it comes to health plans, what you don't know will cost you. On the one hand, you might assume that certain things—like massage therapies—are covered when they're not. Or you might not know that you could have obtained approval for acupuncture treatment that you paid for out-of-pocket. Either way, you're spending money you don't need to spend.

Knowledge of benefits, though, is just the tip of the iceberg in your EOC. There's much more to know if you want to make the most of what you pay for.

Make Sure You're Authorized

In a perfect world, seeing a specialist would be no tougher than getting a manicure. Got a trick knee, weird mole, painful wrist? Pop into the orthopedist's office, or dermatologist's, or sports physician's—and leave half an hour later with a plan of treatment and prescription. No waiting, of course.

Life in the real world, however, is a bit more complicated, particularly if you're in the world of managed care. In most cases, prior authorization is a must. Your primary care physician has to examine that knee, mole or wrist first in order to recommend a specialist. Why? Because your health insurance company wants to ensure that a specific—and usually expensive—medical service or prescription drug is actually necessary, and that it is obtained from the appropriate in-network healthcare provider. If you don't follow the authorization procedure outlined in your EOC, you'll be on the hook for payment.

In general, the following services will require prior authorization:

- Diagnostic procedures (MRI, ultrasound, etc.)
- Brand name medications, if a less-expensive generic equivalent is available
- Medications not on your insurance company's drug formulary
- Surgeries
- Braces/orthotics/prosthetics
- Genetic testing
- Organ transplants
- Physical rehabilitation devices
- Home care services

And, in general, you should follow these five steps for obtaining your doctor's okay:

1) Make sure your doctor knows your service requires authorization.

2) Ask your doctor to contact your insurance company to obtain or verify approval.

3) Make sure your doctor completes the requisite forms for the insurance company.

4) Contact your insurance company to ensure there are no other necessary steps, such as submitting referral slips.

5) Schedule the service only after you are sure authorization has been granted.

> **Following the rules: Christopher's story**
>
> *Having had chronic lower-back pain for six months, Christopher saw his doctor, who recommended an MRI to check for spinal stenosis, disc bulges or spinal tumors. Christopher reminded his doctor that MRIs required prior authorization, so she agreed to contact the insurance company. Two days later she called with the approval, and the insurance company also called to affirm the MRI approval and tell Christopher about in-network radiology centers in his area. After scheduling his appointment for the following Monday, Christopher received his MRI and was responsible for a 20% co-insurance payment.*

Timing Is Everything

Healthcare plans are combinations of two things: annual payments and annual benefits. As a general rule, the sooner in the year you take care of the first—namely, your deductible—the easier it will be to take advantage of the second.

Here's what I mean by that. As you know, your annual deductible is the amount you pay out-of-pocket before your insurance begins to cover your medical claims. Once you've covered the deductible—usually about $500—all you pay for medical services is the standard copayment and co-insurance. Furthermore, once you reach your maximum out-of-pocket limit—usually about $3,000—then the insurance company picks up 100% of the medical tab.

For many reasons, then, it makes sense to get the pain over with and spend your deductible early in the year. Financially, of course, the outlay is the same, whether you pay your deductible early or not. Psychologically, however, there's freedom in knowing you're "done" with your expenses. And that translates into physical benefits as well, since you're then more likely to seek health services when you know you're paying less for them.

> *Caveat:* If you're on a limited budget and paying a high deductible, you're likely to avoid seeking services at all. Check Chapter Two and make sure you're not cheating yourself of health benefits with an unrealistic deductible.

What's more, certain services should be performed at the beginning of the year to identify any health issues that might require on-going medical care. And, if that's not motivation enough, keep in mind that if you don't take advantage of these during the calendar year, then you have to wait until the following year—at which point, of course, you'll have to pay another deductible and series of copayments and co-insurance payments.

Below are typical "use it or lose it" annual benefits:

- Physical exams
- Mammograms
- Prostate exams
- Eye exams
- Dental cleaning

And here are typical "limited visit" benefits, in which your insurance typically pays for a certain number of visits annually:

- Physical therapy
- Mental health therapy
- Acupuncture
- Chiropractic care

To sum up: *The earlier you reach your deductible and copayment maximum, the better you can take advantage of your medical benefits.* And here's how you can maximize those benefits before the year is out:

1) Make sure the last check has cleared on your deductible before scheduling further medical services. If the insurance company doesn't have proof that the deductible is fully paid, you may find yourself paying for a service and then applying for a refund.

2) Leave yourself enough time before the end of the year to schedule limited-visit services, like physical therapy. If your plan allows for 12 visits and you only have two weeks left on the plan, you'll end up having to scrap most of the benefit.

3) Schedule any appointments that may not be covered the following year if you're planning to change plans or cut back on coverage.

4) Order a 90-day supply of prescription drugs in December so that you're covered for the first quarter of the following year.

The eyes have it: Greg's story

Greg's insurance plan had a $300 deductible that applied to all medical services, including vision. In fact, Greg discovered that even prescription glasses counted toward the deductible. This was true even though the insurance company did not "cover" the cost of glasses—that is, Greg would not be reimbursed for prescription glasses if he submitted a receipt. Therefore, Greg made it a point every January to buy new prescription glasses and apply the cost to the plan's deductible, thereby killing two expenses—the glasses and the deductible—with one payment.

Timing is everything: Larry uses his benefits wisely

Larry had had his share of medical issues throughout the year. It was now early November and he needed hip surgery, in which a full recovery would require 12 weekly physical therapy treatments. Although he had met his $500 annual deductible and had used six of his 12 covered physical therapy visits, he wasn't sure he'd met his $3,000 annual copayment maximum. And he was tapped out financially. Immediate surgery did not seem like an affordable option.

Fortunately, Larry had only $150 left on his annual copayment total, which meant he could have his hip surgery in November and pay nothing more than amount. He then took advantage of his six remaining physical therapy visits and paid an additional $360 for six more sessions starting in January, applying that amount to his annual deductible.

By having his surgery before the end of the year, Larry saved $1,350. Had he waited until January, the copay-

ments for the surgeon, anesthesiologist and surgery center would have been $1,500—instead of the $150 he ended up paying to meet his copayment limit for the previous year.

In Summary: The Least You Need to Know

Reading your insurance plan is one thing. *Applying* it is another, and one that sometimes requires skill in tweaking its benefits and limitations to fit your needs. If you're facing a fairly serious—i.e., expensive—health issue, *and you have time to plan a course of action*, spend a little time in working the timing, authorizations and benefits to your situation.

- RTM—Read The Manual. Get to know your Evidence of Coverage so you can maximize your benefits.

- Never skip the authorization process.

- The sooner you meet your deductible, the less you'll worry about your health and expenses. Get your "musts"—like new glasses or physical exams—out of the way early.

- Remember to schedule your "lose it or lose it" benefits before year-end.

- Schedule limited-visit benefits, like physical therapy, well before the year—and the benefits—run out.

<<>>

Chapter Five:
You Better Shop Around

Most people would agree: Hiring a plumber is pretty straightforward. You ask your friends who they use, you find out what they paid, you make a few calls, and you hire the one who seems to give the best service at the best price.

Hiring a doctor—that's another story. In fact, we don't even say "hiring." We say we're "going to" the doctor's office, as if we're going to a church or temple or some other place of higher purpose, where money is simply a matter beneath discussion.

Well, it's time to take the reverence out of hiring a doctor. As with other professions, service and cost among medical doctors can vary widely. Smart consumers need to take time to figure out which doctor fits their needs and wallet, and smarter consumers will do that before a real health need arises.

How to Pick a Doctor

I'm all about controlling healthcare costs. Therefore I recommend not using cost as a guide for picking a doctor. Here's why: If you don't see a good doctor, you'll spend even more money fixing your health problem and looking for a better doctor.

So how do you pick a good doctor? Here are some tips:

- *Ask a doctor.* Healthcare professionals are the best assessors of other healthcare professionals. I asked my dentist which doctor he uses because I like the way he takes care of me as a patient.

- *Ask a friend.*

- *Research online.* Find professional and personal reviews, community involvement and other examples of this person's reputation.

- *Look for affiliations* with teaching hospitals and universities.

- *Look for affiliations* with other talented colleagues that your prospective doctor may have learned from or practiced with.

- *Check for membership* in trade organizations or associations, particularly those that advocate for better patient care.

- *Use intuition.* Is this doctor trying to up-sell services, talk over you, dismiss your problems, make questionable recommendations? I once left a doctor because I didn't get a good feeling from her disorganized office and dusty rug.

Remember that a good doctor will always give you a feeling of confidence and trust. If you leave an office feeling confused, misunderstood or uncertain, it's time to look for another doctor.

Doctor X vs. Doctor Y

Here's a medical truth: Healthcare providers can charge different rates for the same medical services. Let's say, for instance, that Doctor X's office on 2300 Park View charges $110 for a standard office visit, while Doctor Y's office on 2000 Park View charges $180 for the same visit. Does this mean Doctor Y is better? Not necessarily. (But you can certainly check Yelp! or other online resources for reviews.) Should you see Doctor X to save money? That depends.

If you're part of a network, government program or PPO, cost isn't relevant. If you're a Medicaid patient, Medicaid would pay either doctor $45 and you would pay nothing. Similarly, Medicare, the federal program for seniors and the disabled, would pay each doctor $60. An HMO or PPO would pay each doctor an "allowed amount"--say $75—and you, as the network member, would simply pay the standard copayment.

But let's say Doctors X and Y are out of your network, or that they don't accept Medicaid, Medicare or any insurance at all. That's when price really does matter. If you pay cash, you would likely receive a 20%-25% discount, which would bring the out-of-pocket cost to about $90 for Doctor X and $135 for Doctor Y—a $45 difference for what is likely the same service. Or, if

Doctors X and Y are out of network, the network would still pay its allowed amount of $75, but you'd be responsible for the balance. In that case, Doctor X would take $45 from your wallet and Doctor Y would take $105—a $60 difference in cost.

So, do a little homework:

- *Call* your insurance provider to see if the doctor is in your network or accepts your insurance.

- *Call* the doctor's office to see what they will accept in payment.

- *Check* Yelp! and other online services for patient reviews.

Talk With Your Doc

Rare is the office visit that doesn't involve something more than an office visit. Blood tests, urine tests, X-rays, MRIs, endoscopies, referrals, procedures, surgery—the list of "we need..." goes on and on. Naturally, these health services come with a price, and that price can swing widely from office to office.

Particularly if you don't have insurance, endless testing can be a terrifying prospect. One blood sample can cost as much as a new microwave; a colonoscopy can be more expensive than a leather sofa. But yes, you can have your health and your wallet, too.

Having the discussion

Use due diligence for services your doctor might recommend, such as X-rays, referrals to specialists, scans or other procedures. First and foremost, *tell your doctor your financial situation.* Then, ask the following questions.

- How much are these services?

- Might you recommend more of these services in the future?

- Would my health condition improve without these services?

- Would my condition improve with a less expensive alternative treatment?

- Can I hold off on these services (or have them done sooner) in order to take advantage of my insurance deductible?

- Can you refer me to providers who are within my health insurance network?

Those tests!

When you hear those three words—"You need tests"—first, establish clearly in your own mind that these tests are necessary. Ask your doctor:

- What would the tests reveal?

- Are there less expensive tests that would be just as effective?

- Have these tests already been done? (Make sure your doctor has a detailed copy of all previous medical records and test results.)

- Are these tests covered by my insurance?

- Is the testing center in my insurance network?

- Can I shop around for other testing centers that may be less expensive?

More legwork = less hassle

Finally, a little legwork outside the doctor's office might pay off big time. Let's say your doctor recommends an MRI on your knee at a nearby hospital. Here's what you can do:

- *Call* the hospital and other MRI providers in your area and ask, not for price, but for *what they will accept in payment.*

- *Check* Medicare reimbursement rates to benchmark the cost of an MRI. The Medicare program has fee schedules for reimbursement rates for doctors, hospitals and other healthcare providers, and those schedules are used by insurance companies to negotiate payment rates. You'll find them at www.cms.gov/Medicare.

- *Check* the hospital's website for its MRI co-payment information. Hospitals often list co-payment information by insurance company.

- *Use* your insurance company's cost estimator tool to estimate your payment for an MRI. You can also use this tool to calculate payments for other procedures, treatments or health conditions.

- *Compare* costs of MRIs and other services on these consumer websites:
    - www.lifehappens.org
    - www.healthcarebluebook.com
    - www.fairhealthconsumer.org

Getting the picture: Lisa's story

Lisa had been out of work for two years, had just moved to a new city and had no medical, dental or vision insurance. She noticed her vision getting worse and knew she needed an eye examination and prescription glasses.

Using the Internet, Lisa learned that a standard eye exam should cost about $65 and that glasses would cost another $150. She then checked for online reviews of local optometrists, found three with high ratings, and called each for prices. One charged $60 for and exam and $200 for glasses; another charged $90 for an exam and $120 for glasses, and the third had a package deal of $185 for both. Given the favorable reviews for all three, Lisa picked the third optometrist and saved about $50.

In-Network vs. Out-of-Network

It happens all the time: Someone gets insurance—maybe for the first time—goes to a doctor confident that he or she is "covered," and then *bam*, here comes a big bill. For instance:

> **"I won't do THAT again": Leticia's story**
>
> With her first job, Leticia received her first health insurance policy. She got sick, went to the doctor, and was handed a bill for $150—the full amount for the doctor's visit.
>
> She asked her insurance company what happened, and found she'd gone to an out-of-network doctor. An in-network doctor would have accepted the network's allowed amount of $100 per visit, and Leticia would have been responsible for a copayment of just $20 - 20% of that amount. As it was, her insurance company paid just 40% of the billed amount, which was $60. Leticia was on the hook for the rest: $90.
>
> **Lesson learned:** Next doctor visit, Leticia would go in-network and save $70.

Leticia was lucky: She paid only $70 in what financial guru Dave Ramsey would call a "stupid tax." Just imagine if she'd taken an overnight stay in an out-of-network hospital, or had a series of tests in an out-of-network lab. At that point, the "stupid tax" might run into thousands of dollars.

But sometimes staying in-network isn't as easy as it looks. If you're having surgery, for instance, it's common that the surgeon will be in your network, but the anesthesiologist or radiologist might not.

So take the following steps to minimize your financial impact:

- *Ask* your doctor to list *all* the healthcare providers in your surgery, not just the surgeon.

- *Check* the insurance company's directory for the names of those providers.

- *Avoid* unpleasant surprises by *calling* the providers to ensure they're still participating in your network.

- *Find* in-network providers, with the help of your doctor, if you learn that some of the recommended providers are out-of-network, or

- *Negotiate* acceptable rates from any non-network providers.

- *Submit* bills from those out-of-network providers to your insurance company, *before* you pay anything. Your insurance company may pay something, and you might be able to negotiate the remaining balance with the provider.

But who says all health services have to take place in a doctor's office or hospital, anyway? For some money-saving options on services and surgeries, check the next chapter.

Concierge Medicine vs. Same Old

As the name implies, concierge medicine offer a more personalized approach to healthcare. Instead of being one patient among thousands (physicians in regular practice often oversee 2,000 patients), a concierge patient is one among only 300 to 600. Same-day or next-day appointments are the norm (nationally, the average wait time is 20 days), wait times are nonexistent (instead of an average 27 minutes), and consultations are regularly a half-hour instead of an average of eight minutes. Naturally, the result is overall better health. A recent study showed that patients under this personalized care experience 65% fewer hospitalizations than like-age patients in the standard health system

The downside, not surprisingly, is price. Annual fees for a concierge health membership are $195 to $5,000 per year, in addition to fees per service. Some practices are cash-only, and few accept insurance. Because each concierge practice is individual, consult several to find out how each structures its pricing and procedures.

> **Situation: More money than time**
>
> *Jennifer is a successful divorce attorney who's in general good health, but requires regular oversight of her blood pressure and type 2 diabetes. Particularly when she works a heavy caseload, she skips doctor appointments rather than spend hours wait-*

ing for a consultation. Although she knows she's only postponing trouble, immediate client needs outweigh her non-emergency health needs, and she's made it her "policy" to walk out after waiting more than 20 minutes to see a doctor.

Solution: Concierge services

Jennifer discovered a concierge health center in the upscale shopping mall just steps away from her office building. Her secretary can schedule same-day appointments, allowing her to step in for a half-hour during a lunch break for a quick consultation. As a result, her blood pressure is at its lowest point in several years, her weight has improved, and she's begun to reverse her diabetic condition.

Why go:

- Quality physician care
- No wait times
- Same-day or next-day appointments
- Longer, more personalized consultations
- Customized wellness programs
- Less harried, less stressed healthcare environment

When to go:

- Physical checkups
- Monitoring chronic conditions
- Screenings
- Nutrition/health consultations
- Minor illnesses/ailments
- Detailed follow-up plans

When not to go:

- Medical emergencies that require ER attention
- Non-membership

In Summary: The Least You Need To Know

- Doctor visits and lab tests vary widely by price.

- Ask for cash discounts when you're out-of-network or uninsured.

- Check policies to see if tests, lab work and X-rays are covered.

- Make sure you know why you need recommended tests and health services.

- Investigate less expensive options.

- Stick to the network wherever possible.

- For an annual fee, concierge services deliver personalized healthcare in a low-stress environment

<<>>

Chapter Six: Healthcare A La Carte

It used to be that going to the doctor meant going to the doctor—the one man (and it usually was a man) who weighed your newborns, bandaged your kid's ankle, diagnosed your strep throat and even delivered your babies. Even today, it's a nice thing to have at least one doctor who knows you and your family and remembers the last time you came in with that case of hives.

For most of us, though, going to *the* doctor simply isn't possible, or practical, for that matter. We all have different types of health situations and need different kinds of services. And while we might wish for some doctor/hero to solve all our myriad health needs, in today's day and age we can often get better care—and better pricing—when we know how to tailor our healthcare choices.

So next time you need to see a doctor, take a look at some healthcare options that might be faster, cheaper, and just as good.

Retail Medical Clinic to the Rescue

Situation: It's no big deal

Jenny woke up with a severe sore throat. Her doctor's office was closed, and the local ER had a three-hour wait.

Solution: Retail clinics

Jenny called a local retail clinic and learned that wait time for an appointment was just 15 minutes. She arrived and was seen by a nurse practitioner within 12 minutes. She received an exam and culture test for strep throat. The test came back negative; she received a non-prescription drug and recovered at home in a few days.

Savings: $55 and three hours. The retail clinic co-payment was just $20, versus $40 for urgent care and $75 for the ER—which, of course, had a much longer wait time.

In other words, retail medical clinics are great options when you're sick or injured enough to need attention, but not necessarily urgent attention. They're actual medical clinics, staffed by qualified medical professionals, and located in pharmacies, supermarkets and retail stores. They can handle sore throats, earaches, sprains, infections—just about any minor medical need.

Why go?

- Staffed by qualified nurse practitioners, physician assistants, and sometimes doctors

- Accredited by state organizations and agencies
- Care equal to doctor's office, according to studies
- Convenient—no appointments, slight wait time
- Dispenses common medications
- Treats wide range of conditions
- Provides follow-up care
- Often has relationship with local doctor
- Affordable and accepts health insurance

When to go:

- Earaches, headaches
- Urinary tract infections
- Upper respiratory infections
- Cold, flu, sore throat, bronchitis
- Rashes and other skin conditions
- Cuts, lacerations, sutures removed
- Sprain
- Blood pressure check
- Immunizations and vaccinations
- Screenings and tests for some conditions

When not to go (and head to an ER instead):

- Infant medical care
- X-rays
- Severe pain, injury or bleeding

Where to go:

- CVS MinuteClinic (www.minuteclinic.com)
- Walgreens Take Care Clinic (www.takecarehealth.com)
- Target Clinic (www.target.com/pharmacy/clinic-home)
- To locate other retail clinics in your area: Convenient Care Association (www.ccaclinics.org)

Urgent Care Center vs. Emergency Room

What brings most people to emergency rooms? Panic. It's worth remembering that 65% of visits to emergency rooms are not actually true emergencies. They can be handled at urgent care centers with the same quality outcomes and at much lower costs. Sometimes called walk-in clinics, these urgent care centers are medical facilities staffed by doctors that offer immediate medical services for treatment of minor illnesses and injuries.

> **Situation: It's a bigger deal**
>
> Twelve-year-old Billy banged up his arm and ankle on a major skateboard fall. Mom realized he probably needed stitches on his arm and a possible X-ray on the ankle. No stranger to emergency medical care (she had two other young boys), Mom had to decide whether Billy's fall required ER attention.

Solution: Urgent Care Center

Mom decided to take Billy to the urgent care center close to the skateboard park, where an X-ray revealed that his ankle was not broken, just badly sprained. An attending physician put 15 stitches in Billy's arm, which were removed 10 days later at the center at no follow-up cost.

Savings: $110 and several hours. *Because the family had met its insurance deductible, Mom was charged only $40 for the urgent care visit. An ER visit would have cost $150-plus with her insurance plan, and would likely have meant several hours of waiting.*

Be aware, too, that if your condition requires more urgent attention, the doctors and nurses at the clinic will send you to the nearest ER—and they'll call to let the hospital know you're coming.

Why go:

- Big savings. The average cost of a hospital ER visit is $1,250, and the average insurance copayment is $75. The average urgent care center charges $150, and the average insurance copayment is $40.
- Professional medical personnel (often ER doctors)
- Convenient—no appointment, short wait time
- Dispenses common prescription drugs
- Provides follow-up care
- Accepts insurance

When to go:

- Urinary tract infections
- Allergies and rashes
- Insect bites
- Lower back pain
- Headaches
- Earaches
- Cold, flu, sore throat
- Bronchitis
- Sprains
- Cuts and lacerations
- X-rays

When not to go (and head to an ER instead):

- Infant medical care
- Serious illnesses or injuries

Surgery Center vs. Hospital

For many people, the word "surgery" means "hospital." It means crowded waiting rooms, gurneys, hallways, nurses waking you at night to dispense your sleeping medication.

But for outpatient surgery, it doesn't have to mean that anymore. Today more than 50% of elective minor surgeries take place at free-standing medical facilities that not only provide excellent service, but also cost significantly less than a hospital procedure.

Situation: It's complicated

After a number of doctor visits for foot problems, Gary was told he needed surgery. His surgeon worked at both the local hospital and local surgery center. Both recommended facilities were in his network—but the anesthesiologist at the surgery center was not. The dilemma: Pay the bigger co-pay for hospital, where the anesthesiologist was in network? Or pay more for the anesthesia at the surgery center? So Gary did the math (see calculations below) and found that his overall cost would be $120 more if he had the surgery performed at the surgery center.

Gary's Copayments	Hospital	Surgery Center	Savings (Cost)
Facility Copay	$1,100	$500	$600
Surgeon Copay	$180	$180	$ -
Anesthesia Charge	$180	$900	($720)
Gary Pays	$1,460	$1,580	*($120)*

So Gary informed his surgeon of the additional cost he'd incur by having the surgery at the surgery center.

Solution:

Because the quality of care was the same, hospital versus surgery center came down to a numbers game. Gary's surgeon helped him negotiate a rate with the anesthesiologist—who agreed to accept the same copayment amount that Gary would have paid for anesthesia at the hospital.

Gary's cost to have his surgery at the surgery center was now well below what it would be to have his surgery at the hospital. Gary saved $600 (see calculations below).

Gary's Copayments	Hospital	Surgery Center	Savings
Facility Copay	$1,100	$500	$600
Surgeon Copay	$180	$180	$ -
Anesthesia Charge	$180	$180	$ -
Gary Pays	$1,460	$860	<u>$600</u>

Why go:

- Shorter wait time
- Convenient locations
- Fewer issues with infections
- Same surgeons as local hospitals (in most cases)
- Backup plans for hospital transfers, if necessary

When to go:

- Colonoscopies and endoscopies
- Pain management
- Orthopedic procedures
- Minor foot surgeries
- Hernia repair
- Biopsies
- Infertility procedures
- Tonsil removal and ear-tube surgeries
- Many eye surgeries, including cataract removal, retinal repair and cornea transplants

When not to go:

- Surgeries that require overnight stays
- Infant procedures

What you could save (examples):

Procedure	Hospital	Surgery Center	Difference	Your Savings*
Colonoscopy	$2,900	$1,050	$1,850	$370
Endoscopy	$3,150	$825	$2,325	$465
Hernia Repair	$4,100	$1,325	$2,775	$555
Tonsils Removal	$5,750	$2,135	$3,615	$723

* Based on a 20% co-insurance

In Summary: The Least You Need to Know

Clearly, then, it's worth putting on your consumer hat when you're in need of patient care. Unless you have a heroic family physician—the type who can treat all your ills and slip in a little homespun wisdom on the side—you're often better off exploring the variety of clinics, specialty centers and skilled medical practitioners available to treat every kind of health need. As a patient/consumer, choice is your friend. Use it wisely to find the best care at a cost that works for you.

- 65% of emergency-room visits are non-emergency.

- Retail clinics can take on most non-serious ailments at lower cost and less wait time.

- Urgent-care centers handle accidents and illnesses with quality care, little wait time and lower cost.

- Surgical centers manage outpatient surgery with identical care as hospitals—and at much lower co-pay.

- Colonoscopies, endoscopies, X-rays and other procedures can be conveniently scheduled at surgical centers.

<<>>

Chapter Seven: Prescription Drug Options

Long hospital stays, state-of-the art lab equipment, round-the-clock nursing care—that's usually what we picture when we talk about big-bucks healthcare expenses. Far and away, though, the biggest medical dollar drain is found in low-tech bottles with childproof caps. Even if you never need an operation or hospital stay, at some point you'll need prescription drugs—and you'll need a way to pay for them.

More and more, drugs are doing the impossible when it comes to health. Drugs can lower blood pressure, control cholesterol, regulate serotonin levels, fight infections, soothe skin inflammations, prevent scores of diseases, improve white-blood cell counts, stop bacterial onslaughts, destroy cancer cells, balance hormones—you name a physical condition, and there's likely a drug that addresses it, or a pharmaceutical company that's working on it.

That's the good news. The bad news is the cost. Almost all new drugs are radically expensive, partly because of the expensive research involved, and partly because—at least initially—there are no competing drugs in the marketplace. (Generic drugs, which use the same formulation as the brand-name drugs, become available only after the brand-name drug has been on the market for 20 years.)

The other bad news is that the older one gets, the more likely one needs those expensive drugs. That means limited or fixed incomes often coincide with rising health costs. And while Medicare and Obamacare can help with prescription drug coverage, the expense can still be overwhelming. For instance:

> **Prescription drug spiral: Lee's story**
>
> *Not long ago, Lee J., an older friend with part-time income and full-time health problems, told me: "The monthly cost of our prescription drugs began to take a toll on our finances, topping $200 per month. The problem was that we didn't have enough prescription drug coverage and my wife was put on an expensive blood thinner. We needed help and didn't know where to start."*

So here's the good news. It's not hard to take action and bring down your prescription drug costs, and you don't necessarily have to sort through dozens of different prescription plans to do it. Here's where to start.

Check Your Coverage

Even if you don't currently need prescription drugs, don't let yourself get caught short. Check your health insurance policy for its "tiered formulary," which lists all approved medications and their copayments. When possible, you'll want to choose the lowest-cost formulary that has the lowest copayments and contains generic medications. You'll also want to give your doctor a copy of that formulary to make sure you're getting appropriate prescription drugs.

Sometimes choosing the right drug at the right co-payment can be a kind of Goldilocks-and-the-Three-Bears experience, where you'll have to try various options before you hit the one that's "just right." For instance:

> **Change for the cheaper: Alex's story**
>
> For five years, Alex managed his chronic acid reflux with Nexium, which was a "tier two" drug on his insurance policy, costing a $25 copayment for a monthly supply. The insurance company then decided to bump Nexium to tier three (the highest level), which would bring the cost to $45 per month.
>
> Alex didn't want to pay the extra $20 per month, so he checked other options on the formulary. On tier two, his insurance company offered Prilosec, a similar drug, that cost $25 per month. Tier one offered Omeprazole, a generic version of Prilosec, for $10 per month. Alex tried Omeprazole for three months, wasn't happy with the results, and then tried Prilosec. Prilosec controlled his symptoms, and the new formulary enabled Alex to maintain his $25 co-pay.

When Possible, Go Generic

Like many other inventions, newly invented drugs are patent-protected for 20 years. After that, competing pharmaceutical companies can manufacture "generic" versions of that drug, which have the same active ingredients, strength, purity, quality and dosage as the brand-name drug. In fact, the main difference is in the name of the drug—and the price. Frequently, generic drugs cost a fraction of the original patented drug.

> *Caveat: Some patients—see Alex, above—feel that brand-name drugs perform better than the generics. Science, however, says the drugs are exactly the same. Who's right? My opinion: Whatever feels right for your health is the right drug for you.*

Not only are the generic drugs cheaper than brand-name drugs (usually $5-$25 per prescription, compared to $65-$250), they also have much lower co-payment requirements. Co-pays range from $4-$10 for generic prescription drugs, versus $25-$55 for brand-name drugs.

No wonder about half of all prescriptions today are filled with generic drugs. Always ask your doctor if a generic is available for your condition, and if there isn't, see if there's a less-expensive alternative—or even an over-the-counter drug—that she can recommend.

For more information on generic drugs, visit the Food and Drug Administration website at www.fda.gov/cder/ogd.

Generic payoff: Jim and Sheila's story

Jim and Sheila, married 30 years, had reached a healthcare financial crisis. For two years, Sheila had been spending $105 per month on Lipitor to lower her cholesterol. Now Jim needed to take Coumadin to reduce the risk of blood clots after his heart-valve replacement surgery. Since the couple had no prescription drug coverage, that extra $50 per month was the straw that broke the financial bank.

As a less-expensive alternative to Lipitor, Sheila's doctor prescribed Atorvastin calcium, which cost $24 for a monthly supply. He also prescribed a double dosage of 20 milligrams per day (which cost the same as a 10-

millgram dosage) and told Sheila to cut the pills in half. Meanwhile, Jim's doctor prescribed Warfarin sodium as an alternative to Coumadin, which cost only $5 per month and was equally effective.

Result*: Instead of paying $155 per month for their drugs, Jim and Sheila were now spending $17 monthly—$12 for Sheila's Atorvastin calcium and $5 for Jim's Warfarin sodium. The savings added up to $1,650 per year—about 5% of their fixed income!*

Do Some Pharmacy Shopping

Not all pharmacies are the same when it comes to pricing drugs. For example, a high blood-pressure medication can cost a $25 copayment monthly at some traditional chains and pharmacies, but at Costco, a year's supply can be just $35—for a very healthy $265 annual savings.

What's more, many pharmacies also offer discount generic prescription drug programs. Here's a sample:

- Walmart Generics Program (www.walmart.com)
- CVS Pharmacy Health Savings Pass (www.cvs.com)
- Kmart Generics Program (www.rxassist.org)
- Target Generics Program (www.sites.target.com)
- Rx Outreach (www.rxoutreach.com)
- Costco (www.costco.com)

> Tip: For long-term medication needs, switch to a mail-order pharmacy. Often, you'll pay the same copayment for a 90-day supply as you would for a 30-day supply from the local pharmacy.

> **Shaving the savings: Back to Alex**
>
> Faced with some financial issues, Alex—our Prilosec user—decided to try lowering his monthly bills, starting with his $25 prescription copayment. He learned he could get a 90-day supply via mail order for $45. The $10 per month savings made a small but helpful difference in his bills, and saved him some drugstore trips as well.

Apply the apps

Here are just a handful of useful apps to help you locate low-cost prescription drugs.

- LowestMed: Compares prescription drug prices at local pharmacies.

- Prescription Saver: Compares prescription drug prices at pharmacies and offers a free drug discount card.

- GoodRx: Compares prescription drug prices at pharmacies and online, and offers access to prices, coupons and savings tips. Also lists pharmacies that offer free or very low cost generic prescription drugs.

- OTC Plus: Provides a list of over-the-counter medications that meet your particular symptoms. Also sends coupons to your smart phone and shows how to read labels on medications.

Find the deals

Government programs, pharmacies and, yes, even pharmaceutical companies offer a variety of ways to save on prescription drugs. Consider taking these bargain-hunting steps:

- *Contact the pharmaceutical company* for rebates, trial offers and discount cards for specific drugs. Rebate offers are typically equal to a copayment of $20-$40, and free trial offers usually cover a 14-day supply.

- *Look at magazine advertising* for coupons or offers from pharmaceutical companies.

- *Ask your doctor* if he has any samples available of your prescription drug. Pharmaceutical companies often distribute generous samples in order to promote their medication.

- *See if you qualify* for patient assistance programs, which offer free or low-cost prescription drugs to people who are unable to pay for them. All pharmaceutical manufacturers participate in these programs, and all have their own eligibility and application requirements. Check these sites for more details:
    - Partnership for Prescription Assistance (www.pparx.org)

- Patient Assistance Program Center (www.rxassist.org)
- Pharmacycard (www.pharmacycard.org)
- Needymeds (www.needymeds.org)
- Xubex (www.xubex.com)
- The Medicine Program (www.themedicineprogram.com)
- RxHope (www.rxhope.com)
- SelectCare Benefits Network (www.myrxadvocate.com)

Remember, you don't have to be low-income to qualify for a break on prescription drug prices. Many times pharmaceutical costs can be out of reach for just about any budget. Here's an example:

> **Help wanted: Sonia's story**
>
> *Sonia was self-employed with minimal insurance (no prescription drug coverage) when she was diagnosed at age 37 with multiple sclerosis. To slow the progress of the disease and minimize symptoms, she was prescribed Betaseron—which came with a price tag of more than $3,000 per month. After some Internet research, she found a program called BetaPlus offered by the Patient Assistance Program Center (www.rxassist.com). She now receives her annual supply of Betaseron at almost no cost to her.*
>
> **Final analysis: Back to Lee**
>
> *Clearly, my friend Lee has a variety of options when it comes to cutting back on his $200 monthly prescription costs. I'd sum it up this way:*
>
> 1. *Always pick a plan with prescription drug coverage. You never know when you'll need it; I can pretty*

much guarantee that at some point you'll be glad you have it.

2. *If you don't have enough coverage, start doing some homework. Dozens of resources are available for finding low-cost and even no-cost medication options. A few hours on the Internet, some paperwork and conversations with the right people can result in thousands of dollars in savings. Your health and your wallet are worth the effort.*

In Summary: The Least You Need to Know

- Prescription drug costs are the main cause of skyrocketing healthcare costs.

- Always have some kind of prescription drug coverage. If you don't need it now, you'll be glad you have it at some point.

- Generic drugs can cost less than half the price of brand-name drugs.

- If generics aren't available, have your doctor recommend a different medication, or even an over-the-counter one.

- Look into prescription drug discount programs offered by pharmacies.

- Check out a variety of apps and websites for recommendations on less-expensive substitutes for prescription drugs.

- Look for discounts and rebates from pharmaceutical companies.

- Ask your doctor if she can safely prescribe a double dose of your drug that you can cut in half.

- Use mail-order pharmacies for maximum savings on ongoing prescriptions.

- Check the Internet for help in receiving experimental or disease-specific drugs.

- For seniors, Obamacare offers help in getting through the "coverage gap" in prescription payments (see Chapter Two).

<<>>

Chapter Eight: Handling Your Medical Bills

> *"I had had prostate surgery and recovered just fine. Then the medical bills and insurance statements started pouring in. Why did I get seven bills? How was I going to reconcile all that with my insurance statements? How could I get the money to pay it all—and how did I even know if it was billed correctly? I needed help but didn't know where to go."*
>
> — *Michael W.*

By now you may have figured out that I love a bargain. That's why this is one of my favorite chapters. This isn't about quality of care, picking the best doctor, or making any other subjective decisions about your health. This is about saving money, period.

Medical procedures can run the gamut from appendectomies to X-rays, but there's one thing they all have in common: they're expensive. And when the bill arrives you might want to get one more procedure just to put the jaw back in your mouth. I well remember my friend Diane's reaction when the first bill arrived after a round of chemotherapy treatment for colon cancer: *"Two hundred and fifty dollars just to put the needle in my arm??"*

I'm not going to get into why medical costs are so high (frankly, that's a book in itself). But I will point out that each medical service, no matter how small—even a couple of Tylenol tablets at the hospital—comes with a price. And even if you have insurance galore you'll want to pay attention to each of those services and prices listed in your bill. That's for three reasons:
1) To discover mistakes and overcharges
2) To control how much you pay
3) To understand what is covered and not covered

Guess what? Up to 80% of medical bills contain some kind of error—and many go unnoticed because patients think it's too hard to figure it out. Trust me, it's not. If you can read a stock page or a credit-card statement, you can make sense of your medical bills. And making sense of them is the first step to keeping them more palatable to your wallet.

What's in Your Bill?

Create your own records first

Before the bill arrives, there's one piece of paper you need to have for every procedure. That's *your own written record of dates, services, medications and visits.* Don't rely on the hospital or doctor to keep accurate track of everything that's happening to you. When you have your own record, you're minimizing the likelihood of paying for services you didn't approve of or receive.

> *Tip: Emotionally and physically, emergency procedures are the most difficult to document with accuracy. Have a "just in case" discussion with a spouse, relative or friend so that someone's keeping track of services and procedures in an emergency.*

Know what's in the paperwork

Besides you and your health provider, there's always a third party involved in your medical procedures: your insurance company. Every time you get a medical bill, you also get a statement from your insurer, called Explanation of Benefits. The EOB lets you know that a medical claim is being processed, and that the insurer will be covering its end of the costs.

A medical bill typically contains the following:

- Date service was received
- Description of service
- Codes that identify services
- Dollar amount charged for services
- Medical fees and services approved (and/or denied) by your insurance company
- Dollar amount the insurance company paid the healthcare provider
- Dollar amount (balance) you owe

The Explanation of Benefits (EOB) lists the following:

- Description of medical services
- Medical services covered by insurance company
- Medical services not covered, and why
- Charges billed by the healthcare provider

- Amount the insurance company paid, and amount not covered
- Amount you owe the health provider—taking into account your copayment and deductible

Once you have *both* your EOB and medical bills in hand, start verifying the information. Make sure the dates, services and costs on the bill match those on the EOB, and that none of it contradicts your own records. Ask yourself:

- Do you recall receiving, or approving of all the lab tests, exams and other services on the bill? Do those match up with what's on the EOB?

- Do the dates of your hospital stays, visits or exams correspond with your records, and with the date on the EOB?

- Are the bill's codes for certain procedures consistent throughout? Are they consistent with the EOB's medical coding?

- Can you get itemized billing for any information that is unclear or questionable?

Learn to Spot Common Billing Errors

Here are some errors to look for:

- *Coding errors (wrong codes for type of service, up-coding)*

- *Overstating number of days of hospital stay*
- *Private room charges for a shared room*
- *Charges for medication you didn't take*
- *Charges for tests and services not performed*
- *Charges for personal items, such as soap, shampoo and clothes*
- *Duplicate charges (double billing)*
- *Miscellaneous unexplained charges*

> Tip: Don't pay anything until you are sure both your bill and EOB are correct.

Never pay for these!

As if you didn't have enough to worry about during your hospital stay, mistakes, errors and neglect can make you even sicker than when you went in. Hospital-related illnesses and injuries are known as Hospital Acquired Conditions and Never Events. Your insurance company won't pay for them, and neither should you. So, if you acquire any of the following conditions, keep in mind that the hospital is at fault and must pay for it:

- Bed ulcers
- Catheter infections
- Surgical site infections
- Blood incompatibility problems
- Objects left in body after surgery
- Falls or trauma while in the hospital
- Operating on the wrong body part
- Operating on the wrong patient

A complete list is available from your insurance company.

The Bill is Wrong—Now What?

So let's say you've done all your homework on your medical bill. You matched it to your written records, compared the bill and the EOB, and discovered the following: You've been charged for a prescription you didn't take ($55) and for an extra follow-up visit you didn't have ($145). Here's how to proceed:

- *Gather your written records and statements.* Make sure you have tangible information to show the hospital and insurance company. Particularly if you're being charged for something you *didn't* have, such as an exam, you'll have far more cooperation from the billing department if you can document the services and procedures you *did* have.

- *Immediately contact the health provider's billing department,* and *the insurance provider.* Get your bill and EOB corrected as soon as possible after receiving it. If you wait for the medical provider to call you for nonpayment, you won't get a sympathetic ear about your billing complaints.

- *Get a revised copy of the corrected bill and EOB.*

- *Pay nothing until you have both corrected statements.*

Of course, all that works great if the billing department agrees with your assessment. But let's take human nature into account: Nobody likes to admit a mistake, and you can assume that's doubly true of people who work in billing and collections. Moreover, the bigger the money involved in the dispute, the more temperatures rise on both sides. So if you *know* you're right about an error in your bill, *keep your cool, be persistent, and hang in to the end.*

> **The $3,000 mea culpa: Donna and Paul's story**
>
> *During a CAT scan, a doctor noticed that Donna's uterus showed a vague spot—something that could be either a simple cyst or malignant tumor. Either way, an operation was necessary. The surgeon said that she could remove a cyst in a relatively simple procedure, but wanted permission to perform a hysterectomy in the event of a malignancy. Donna and Paul agreed, and they and the surgeon signed a billing estimate ranging from $3,000 (for routine cyst removal) to $6,300 (for complications or a hysterectomy). Because the surgeon was out-of-network, Donna and Paul would have to pay for the surgery out-of-pocket, and then submit the bill to their insurance company for partial reimbursement.*
>
> *Emerging from the operating room, the surgeon said that "everything went great," the surgery was completely routine, and that a simple cyst was removed from the uterus. Nevertheless, Donna and Paul received a bill for $6,000, the high end of the estimate. When Paul called to question the amount, the surgeon's bookkeeper accused Paul of "calling us liars" and hung*

up on him twice. Paul persisted by submitting a copy of the signed estimate, along with a written account of the pre-surgery conversation and post-operation discussion. He then called to make sure the accountant received the information and politely asked if she'd had time to look it over. Soon after, the accountant apologized for her brusqueness and sent Paul and Donna a revised bill for $3,300.

The insurance company won't pay. Now what?

One person's essential medical procedure is another person's luxury—at least, according to many insurance disputes. For instance:

- Your doctor says you need eyelid surgery to correct a defect. The insurance company says it's cosmetic.

- You have a plastic surgeon put in stitches after an operation. The insurance company says the attending surgeon should have done it.

- You schedule a general anesthesia for a dental procedure. The insurance company wants to pay for a local.

In each case, you have to provide your side of the story *in writing,* outlining exactly why this procedure falls into a category covered by your insurance policy. Make sure your doctor can back you up as to the medical necessity of a procedure.

And don't give up if your appeal is denied. Request a review by an outside, independent review board.

Your EOB or your insurance company can provide a list of independent review organizations.

> ### Case closed: Michael's story
>
> *Bewildered by his post-surgery medical bills, Michael came to me to sort out his paperwork and figure out how to pay what he owed. By comparing Michael's EOB and medical bills with a record of his medical services, we found several errors:*
>
> - *Denied coverage for radiology services (reversed on appeal)*
>
> - *Coding errors by the anesthesiologist and surgeon (confirmed through itemized billing statements; revised and re-billed accordingly, with revised EOB's as well)*
>
> - *Unwarranted charge for private hospital room (revised upon appeal, with revised bill and EOB issued)*
>
> *Together, those errors added up to $1,175 in Michael's favor. Moreover, we negotiated the amount Michael owed on his bills, saving him an additional $1,870. Here's a breakdown of how Michael shaved more than $3,000 off his surgery costs.*
>
> | | Error? | Savings | Negotiated? | % Discount | Savings | Total Savings |
> |---|---|---|---|---|---|---|
> | Physician | No | $ - | Yes | 30% | $125 | $125 |
> | Oncologist | No | $ - | Yes | 15% | $235 | $235 |
> | Radiology Ctr | Yes | $720 | Yes | 20% | $455 | $1,175 |
> | Radiologist | No | $ - | Yes | 25% | $130 | $130 |
> | Surgeon | Yes | $45 | Yes | 30% | $625 | $670 |
> | Anesthesia | Yes | $95 | Yes | 20% | $300 | $395 |
> | Hospital | Yes | $315 | No | 0% | $ - | $315 |
> | TOTAL | | $1,175 | | | $1,870 | $3,045 |

Don't Wait—Negotiate

You wouldn't think of buying a car without negotiating a price—or of replacing a lawn, putting in a pool, or buying a truckload of furniture. Any time you need an expensive item or service, you can bet you'd look around for the best value.

So why not do it with medical bills? Granted, surgeons are not car dealers. But if you're having a cosmetic procedure, out-of-network service or elective surgery—or if you just don't have enough insurance for a necessary operation or hospital stay—you're going to be digging deep into your wallet. You owe it to yourself to get the best care at the best price.

Here's how to proceed:

- *Have the information on hand.* Know the standard costs of the procedures, how much might be covered by insurance, and how much would come out of pocket.

- *Start negotiating well before you actually need the procedure.* After all, you don't pay $25,000 for a Honda and then complain to the dealer that your neighbor got the same model for $23,000. *If you really want to lower your medical bill, make sure you research (as much as possible) ahead of time.*

- *Get over your nerves.* Your healthcare provider is a professional, ethically bound to provide quality medical care, and should have your best interests at heart.

- *Speak to the decision-maker.* Some doctors leave cost decisions to their billing managers. Ask to find out who's in charge of setting rates. If you're negotiating the cost of a hospital stay, call the hospital finance manager.

- *Bring up the discussion early in your visit.* Remember, doctors are short on time. Be specific and brief.

- *Know what to ask for.* A 20% to 50% discount is considered reasonable. Start at 50% and work from there.

- *Put some skin in the game.* You'll get the best price if you pay the entire discounted amount up front. The office's biggest billing hassle is in collections, so getting payment out of the way is a win-win for you and the doctor.

- *If you can't afford to pay it all up front,* pay at least some of the amount to demonstrate good faith.

- *Don't create a bidding war.* Saying, "Dr. Wexler can do the operation for $1,500" is insulting to Dr. Smith. You're likely to undermine your efforts.

- *If you can't get a discount, see if you can get a no-interest payment plan.* Make sure it's one that you can afford monthly.

If you need assistance with bill negotiation, or just don't think you have the stomach for it, a number of organizations can help you out with your medical bills. Some may charge a percentage of what they save you, but it could well be worth it.

Here are 10 organizations to consider:

- Rising Medical Services (www.risingms.com)
- Medical Cost Advocates (www.medicalcostadvocates.com)
- ISNET (www.mymedicalnegotiator.com)
- Healthcare Bluebook (www.healthcarebluebook.com)
- NewChoiceHealth, Inc. (www.newchoicehealth.com)
- The Chapman Consulting Group (www.hospitalbillreview.com)
- Billadvocate.com (www.billadvocate.com)
- Patient Advocate Foundation (www.patientadvocate.com)
- Alliance of Claims Assistance Professionals (www.claims.org)
- Smart Medical Consumer (www.smartmedicalconsumer.com)

In Summary: The Least You Need To Know

- Up to 80% of medical bills contain mistakes.

- Make sure you keep your own written records.

- Always compare your bills, your EOB and your own records.

- When you find a mistake, document your proof.

- Don't be shy about negotiating price: A 20% to 50% discount is considered reasonable, especially if you're paying up front.

<<>>

Chapter Nine: The IRS Can Be Your Friend

Like retirement programs, IRS healthcare programs are designed to help you save money at the front end—before you actually need to start paying medical bills. Offering tax-deferred savings plans and tax credits is the government's way of helping you steer money toward healthcare that would otherwise go to your tax bill.

Even before Obamacare, the IRS—yes, the IRS—provided a number of ways to help you pay for healthcare, regardless of your income. Flexible spending accounts, tax deductions, tax credits and retirement account hardship (penalty-free) distributions have helped millions of taxpayers cut their out-of-pocket health costs.

Now Obamacare adds to those tax breaks with its own money-saving programs for consumers. Spend a few minutes scanning through the options, and you could easily shave thousands from your healthcare costs.

Obamacare Premium Tax Credits

For consumers with big needs and small incomes, healthcare is usually last on the list. The Affordable Care Act steps in to help those folks "find" the money to pay for insurance. This tax credit is for people who've already squeezed every dollar for food, rent and clothing.

What it is: For qualified low- and middle-income workers, a portion of federal taxes goes directly to private insurance companies that participate in Obamacare programs. This tax credit helps cover the cost of insurance premiums.

How it works: The credit is available as soon as you enroll in an insurance plan. The total premium you pay depends on which plan you choose and your income. The less you earn, the less you are expected to contribute toward your premiums, and vice versa.

Best benefit: Premium tax credits start going directly to the insurer as soon as you sign up. You don't have to wait until you file taxes in order to claim your tax credit, and you don't need to submit bills for reimbursements.

The catch: If you don't choose to participate in a healthcare plan at all, you will pay a penalty to the government.

Flexible Spending Account

What it is: A savings plan set up by your employer that lets you set aside pre-tax earnings to use for medical expenses.

How it works: Like an IRA, and FSA lets you set aside pre-tax income (up to $2,500 in 2013). After the end of the year, you submit your medical expenses and are reimbursed up to the amount available in your FSA. The account can cover co-pays, deductibles, prescriptions and other out-of-pocket expenses.

Best benefit: An FSA can cover expenses you might not expect. Your employer's program might well include:

- Eye doctor visits, glasses, contact lenses and laser surgeries
- Flu shots and vaccines
- Some non-prescription drugs
- Mileage to and from your doctor's office
- Out-of-town medical care

The catch: If you don't use the full amount of your FSA by the following March, you lose the remaining fund balance. So if you've got $2,000 in the account and find you've spent only $1,500 of it, you need to schedule additional healthcare services to work off the remaining amount. *It's better to claim too much than too little.*

Best for: Consumers who need to save for "known" expenses that aren't covered by insurance, like Susie's braces.

> **Putting the "flexible" in FSA: Stephanie and Tony's story**
>
> Stephanie and Tony have two young children—one with special needs—and two jobs that provide FSA programs. Last year they contributed $3,750 to their FSA programs, but actually incurred almost twice that amount in expenses. This year, they decided to max

> out their FSA accounts to $5,000 (which saved them $1,250 in income tax). However, their medical bills totaled only $4,750, leaving them with $250 in FSA money they would have to either use or lose.
>
> So Stephanie got creative in figuring additional medical bills to submit for reimbursement. She decided to submit mileage and parking costs related to 12 physical therapy sessions she'd had earlier that year ($130), and then scheduled end-of-year flu shots for her and her family ($120). "We were able to pay all our medical bills with tax-free income," she says. "I'm proud of my husband and myself."

Health Savings Account

What it is: A savings and investment plan for medical expenses, offered by employers and banks to consumers with high-deductible insurance policies.

How it works: Unlike an FSA, the unused funds in an HSA can roll over from year to year.

Best benefit: If you don't use up your HSA on medical expenses by age 65, you can withdraw the money tax-free.

The catch: Like any investment, HSAs are subject to market fluctuations, and some also have fees attached. Also, you must have an insurance deductible of at least $1,250 for an individual and $2,500 for a family, and you'll pay taxes on any HSA withdrawals made for non-approved medical expenses.

Best for: People who incur relatively few year-to-year medical expenses and want the security of knowing they have money set aside—and growing—in the event of a true medical necessity.

Income Tax Deduction

What it is: A tax deduction for qualified medical expenses.

How it works: If you paid more than 10% of your adjusted gross income for medical and dental care, you may deduct the amount of expenses that exceeded that 10%. For instance, if you paid $15,000 in hospital bills after a car accident, and your annual adjusted gross income was $75,000, you can deduct $7,500 (the amount of your expenses that exceeds 10% of $75,000) from your income tax.

Best benefit: Makes a bad year slightly easier—because, let's face it, any year is a bad year when medical expenses exceed 10% of your income!

The catch: Not every medical expense counts toward your deduction. Contact your tax accountant for advice and assistance, and check the IRS website (www.irs.gov) to see if you qualify.

Best for: People with lower incomes, little insurance and substantial medical issues.

> **Every little bit helps: Kerry and David's story**
>
> Kerry and David are self-employed with no healthcare insurance and a combined income of $65,000. Last year Kerry had hip surgery and David had heart surgery, which cost them a total of $8,860, or nearly 14% of their total income. Having scraped together the cash to pay the medical expenses, they were grateful they could at least deduct $2,360 ($8,860 minus $6,500) from their income tax that year.

Retirement Account Hardship Distribution

What it is: Withdrawal from your tax-deferred retirement account for an immediate and heavy financial need, which can include medical expenses.

How it works: You must demonstrate to the IRS that your need for the money is pressing and essential and should not be subject to a withdrawal penalty and tax.

Best benefit: You get money when you really need it without paying a fee.

The catch: Not every medical expense qualifies as a genuine hardship, so receiving this distribution can be challenging. And even if you do qualify, you're putting a dent in your retirement savings and risking your financial future.

Best for: A last resort: when medical debts are so overwhelming your financial future is at risk anyway.

> **"Need to find another way": Stan's story**
>
> Stan, age 45, had accumulated about $125,000 in his retirement account when his son fell off a skateboard and suffered brain trauma. Hospitalized for weeks, his son slowly recovered with the help of ongoing physical and occupational therapy, at a cost of tens of thousands of dollars. Stan applied for a hardship distribution to help with the medical bills, but was turned down. The IRS argued—and Stan's accountant agreed—that Stan could get financial help from other resources, such as a home equity loan. A $30,000 loan would have an interest rate of less than 5%; taking $30,000 from his IRA, by contrast, would cost Stan an additional $10,000 in penalties and taxes. Plus Stan would lose a huge chunk from his retirement: that $30,000 would build to more than $200,000 by the time he was 65. Stan didn't like the idea of a loan, so he decided to get a second job as a security guard in order to pay his son's medical bills—and to leave his retirement alone.

In Summary: The Least You Need To Know

Human nature is the biggest obstacle to getting tax breaks. If you're more of a short-term thinker—the type who says, "Oh, we'll figure out how to pay for it when we get there"—you'll likely miss out on a lot of savings. A little long-term planning can make a big difference in your health and your wallet. For more information on healthcare tax breaks, visit the IRS website at www.irs.gov.

- Obamacare tax credits help pay premiums for qualified low- and middle-income wage-earners.

- IRS and employer savings plans—FSAs and HSAs—help you pay off big health bills with minimal financial pinch.

- Income tax breaks help ease the pain of an expensive healthcare year.

- If you're up against the wall with health can finances, withdrawing from your retirement account is a last resort.

- The best way to save money is to be a long-term thinker.

<<>>

Conclusion

Better Healthcare Starts Now!

Health issues aren't like any other financial issues. You plan and save to buy a house or car, or to send a kid to college—but who "saves" for an emergency appendectomy? Or for two nights in an ICU? They might sound like rhetorical questions, but they're not.

Even when you have insurance for those "what ifs," you owe it to yourself and your family to take charge of your health and finances. When you're a smart healthcare consumer, you can rest easy knowing that, whatever happens, you'll be getting the best quality care for the best price.

So be your own healthcare advocate. You've read the book; now start taking action.

Read the policies

Half an hour spent reviewing your coverage can save you hours of aggravation, not to mention hundreds of dollars. Don't wait until you get there to find out how much of a copayment you need for the emergency room, or whether the doctor you're about to see is in your network, or whether you needed authorization for that dermatology visit. If you can remember your niece's birthday, you can remember your coverage essentials.

Pick the right deductible

This is one of the trickiest maneuvers in healthcare. You want a deductible that is high enough to keep down your monthly premium cost, but not so high that you avoid seeking healthcare altogether. If you're young and healthy, you can get away with a high deductible, but if you're older and have children, you must be realistic about the fact that, one way or another, you're going to have to pay for healthcare.

So never let your deductible become more than 5% of your gross income. And for the best deal in healthcare plans, get a job with benefits!

Plan ahead

Next time you're in the supermarket, take a look at the retail health center. While you're driving, make a mental note of the nearest urgent care center. If your knees are giving you problems, don't wait until December to start physical therapy. Planning for the "what ifs" doesn't have to be a full-time job. Simple awareness can make the difference between whether you end up spending money on health services that you could have spent on many other things.

Keep records

Hospitals, doctors' offices and insurance companies make mistakes—and usually not in your favor. Know how much you've spent of your deductible. Keep track of when you've had your annual wellness exams and when you're due again. Make notes of lab tests, blood tests, follow-up visits and hospital services. When you need to argue a bill or show that you don't need that lab test, you'll find the pen is far mightier than your fallible memory. Don't cheat yourself of your money or your consumer rights.

Open your mouth

When you're sick, you're vulnerable. And when you're vulnerable, it's hard to speak up to others—especially the people taking care of you. Remember, though, that health professionals are just that: professionals. They have your best interest at heart, whether it's physical or financial. So be truthful about your health habits and concerns, and be open about your finances. Ask for discounts and payment plans. Ask for generic drugs instead of brand-name. Ask doctors to talk to your insurance company. Stay on your own side.

Do what you can to stay well

Some health issues will always come out of the blue—a car accident, a cancer diagnosis. But many are preventable. If you wear seatbelts and bike helmets, don't text and drive, drink responsibly, quit smoking and curb your junk food habit, you've already saved a bundle on healthcare costs. Healthy people are happier. But healthy and smart people are also prepared for those times when they're less than healthy. Congratulations for being one of them!

<<>>

Helpful Websites

Below is a summary of the recommended Internet websites listed in order as they are presented in this book.

Chapter One: Playing the Insurance Game

- California Department of Managed Healthcare (www.dmhc.ca.gov)
- California Department of Corporations (www.corp.ca.gov)
- California Department of Insurance (www.insurance.ca.gov)
- Medical Board of California (www.californiamedlicense.com)
- California Department of Health Services (www.dhs.ca.gov)
- Obamacare Facts (www.Obamacare.com)
- Center for Medicare and Medicaid Services (www.healthcare.gov)
- U.S. Department of Health and Human Services (www.hhs.org)

Chapter Two: Pick a Plan, Painlessly

(None)

Chapter Three: Government Assistance

- Care Harbor (www.careharbor.org)

- National Association of Free Clinics (www.freeclinics.us)
- Planned Parenthood (www.plannedparenthood.org)
- The HealthWell Foundation (www.healthwellfoundation.org)
- The U.S. Department of Health and Human Services (www.hhs.gov)
- National Cancer Institute (www.cancer.gov)
- American Cancer Society (www.cancer.org)
- Cancer Financial Assistance Coalition (www.cancerfac.org)
- CancerCare (www.cancercare.org)
- The Cancer Support Community (www.cancersupportcommunity.org)
- Association Cancer On-line Resources (www.acor.org)
- American Breast Cancer Foundation (www.abcf.org)
- Avon Foundation (www.avonbreastcare.org)
- Susan G. Komen Foundation (www.komen.org)
- BreastCancer.org (www.breastcancer.org)
- Advanced Breast Cancer Community (www.advancedbreastcancercommunity.org)
- Prostate Cancer Foundation (www.pcf.org)
- Prostate Cancer Info Link (www.prostatecancerinfolink.net)
- Zero: The Project to End Prostate Cancer (www.zerocancer.org)
- Us TOO (www.ustoo.com)
- Prostate Conditions Education Council (www.prostateconditions.org)
- American Diabetes Association (www.diabetes.org/in-my-community/programs)
- Diabeteslocal (www.diabeteslocal.org)

- American Association of Diabetes Educators (www.diabetesselfcare.org)
- National Diabetes Information Clearinghouse (www.diabetes.niddk.nih.gov)
- Charles Ray III Diabetes Association, Inc. (www.cr3.org)
- American Heart Association (www.heart.org and www.hearthub.org)
- Cleveland Clinic Heart Center (www.clevelandclinic.org/heartcenter)
- American College of Cardiology (www.acc.org)
- Mended Hearts, Inc. (www.mendedhearts.org)
- Heart Rhythm Society (www.hrsonline.org)
- National Stroke Association (www.stroke.org)
- American Stroke Association (www.strokeassociation.org)
- The Internet Stroke Center (www.strokecenter.org)
- RTH Foundation (www.rthfoundation.org)
- The Stroke Network (www.strokenetwork.net)
- The National Organization of Rare Disorders (www.rarediseases.org)
- Patient Advocacy Foundation (www.patientadvocate.org)
- Survivorship A-Z (www.survivorshipatoz.org)
- Patient Access Network Foundation (www.panfoundation.org)
- ClinicalTrials.gov (www.clinicaltrials.gov)
- Advocacy for Patients with Chronic Illness, Inc. (www.advocacyforpatients.org)
- Social Security (www.socialsecurity.gov)
- State Medical Assistance (www.medicare.gov)
- Extra Help (www.socialsecurity.gov/i1020)
- Insure Kids Now (www.insurekidsnow.gov)
- Center for Medicaid and Medicare Services (www.cms.gov)

Chapter Four: Get Your Premium's Worth

(None)

Chapter Five: You Better Shop Around

- Life Happens (www.lifehappens.org)
- Healthcare Bluebook (www.healthcarebluebook.com)
- Fair Health Consumers (www.fairhealthconsumer.org)
- Children's Health Insurance Program (www.insurekidsnow.gov)

Chapter Six: Healthcare A La Carte

- CVS MinuteClinic (www.minuteclinic.com)
- Walgreens Take Care Clinic (www.takecarehealth.com)
- Target Clinic (www.target.com/pharmacy/clinic-home)
- Convenient Care Association (www.ccaclinics.org)

Chapter Seven: Prescription Drug Options

- Walmart Generics Program (www.walmart.com)
- CVS Pharmacy Health Savings Pass (www.cvs.com)
- Kmart Generics Program (www.rxassist.org)
- Target Generics Program (www.sites.target.com)
- Rx Outreach (www.rxoutreach.com)
- Costco (www.costco.com)
- Partnership for Prescription Assistance (www.pparx.org)
- Patient Assistance Program Center (www.rxassist.org)
- Pharmacycard (www.pharmacycard.org)
- Needymeds (www.needymeds.org)
- Xubex (www.xubex.com)

- The Medicine Program (www.themedicineprogram.com)
- RxHope (www.rxhope.com)
- SelectCare Benefits Network (www.myrxadvocate.com)
- LowestMed (Software App)
- Prescription Saver (Software App)
- GoodRx (Software App)
- OTC Plus (Software App)

Chapter Eight: Handling Your Medical Bills

- Rising Medical Services (www.risingms.com)
- Medical Cost Advocates (www.medicalcostadvocates.com)
- ISNET (www.mymedicalnegotiator.com)
- Healthcare Bluebook (www.healthcarebluebook.com)
- NewChoiceHealth, Inc. (www.newchoicehealth.com)
- The Chapman Consulting Group (www.hospitalbillreview.com)
- Billadvocate.com (www.billadvocate.com)
- Patient Advocate Foundation (www.patientadvocate.com)
- Alliance of Claims Assistance Professionals (www.claims.org)
- Smart Medical Consumer (www.smartmedicalconsumer.com)

Chapter Nine: The IRS Can Be Your Friend

- Internal Revenue Service (www.irs.gov)

<<>>

Glossary

- <u>Annual Benefits</u>: Medical and healthcare services included in your insurance policy that are free of cost to you (no copayment).

- <u>Appeal</u>: A request made by a healthcare provider or patient to reconsider a denied claim for medical services.

- <u>Benefits</u>: Services and coverage you receive in exchange for payment of your insurance premiums.

- <u>Brand-Name Medications</u>: Prescription drugs identified with a pharmaceutical company brand name.

- <u>Catastrophic Health Insurance Plan</u>: Minimal coverage designed to cover a policy-holder from financial disaster in the event of a serious and expensive medical emergency. It is not designed for day-to-day medical expenses or even emergency room visits.

- <u>Chronic Illness</u>: A health condition or disease that is persistent or otherwise long-lasting in its effects. The term chronic is usually applied when the course of the disease lasts for more than three months.

- Clinical Trials: Medical research and drug development tests that generate safety and efficacy data. They are conducted on human patient volunteers only after satisfactory information has been gathered on the safety of the nonclinical procedures.

- COBRA: The Consolidated Omnibus Budget Reconciliation Act. Requires employers to provide temporary health insurance coverage to those who have lost their jobs.

- Community Assistance Programs: Programs that treat or provide assistance for specific common and/or chronic health conditions, such as heart disease, cancer and diabetes. These programs can be run by local, state and federal governments, and non-profit organizations.

- Concierge Medicine: Concierge medicine enables a patient to receive enhanced, personalized care from a primary care physician in exchange for a retainer or annual fee. Concierge programs vary widely in structure, payment requirements, level of service provided, and fees charged.

- Copayment: The portion that patients pay healthcare providers for obtaining medical services.

- Covered Medical Services (Coverage): Medical services for which a health insurance company pays a significant portion.

- Deductible: The total annual amount you pay before a health insurance company will begin paying claims for most of the medical services you receive.

- Drug Formulary: A collection of formulas for the compounding and testing of medication. The development of prescription formularies is based on evaluations of efficacy, safety and cost-effectiveness of drugs.

- Evidence of Coverage (EOC): A booklet you receive from your health insurance company explaining your health insurance benefits, the medical services that are covered and not covered, your rights and responsibilities, dispute and appeals procedures, where to find in-network healthcare providers, and other information to manage your health insurance benefits.

- Explanation of Benefits (EOB): A document from your health insurance company explaining the amount they paid for the services rendered, any portions not covered and the reasons, and the amount you owe the healthcare provider.

- Fee-For-Service (FFS): A payment model where services are unbundled and paid for separately.

- Flexible Spending Account: An employer-sponsored program in which employees can set aside pre-tax dollars to pay for medical and healthcare expenses.

- Generic Prescription Drugs/Medications: Prescription medications that have the same active ingredients and strength as brand-name drugs and can be sold for less.

- Group Health Insurance: Insurance provided by an employer or organization.

- Health Maintenance Organization (HMO): A managed care program in which doctors and other professionals have agreed by contract to treat patients in accordance with certain guidelines and restrictions in exchange for a steady stream of customers.

- Healthcare Providers: Physicians, hospitals, surgery centers, medical clinics and other healthcare professionals that provide healthcare and medical services.

- Health Savings Account (HSA): A tax-advantaged medical savings account available to taxpayers enrolled in high-deductible health plans. Unlike a flexible spending account (FSA), funds roll over and accumulate year to year if not spent.

- High Deductible Health Plan: A health insurance plan with lower premiums and higher deductibles than a traditional health plan.

- Hospital Acquired Conditions (HAC) / Never Events: HACs are avoidable conditions that could reasonably have been prevented. Such conditions are not present when patients are admitted to a hospital, but occur during the course of the stay. Never Events are serious and costly errors in the provision of health care services that should never happen.

- Individual Health Insurance: Health insurance plans available for purchase by an individual for herself and/or her family for medical and healthcare expenses.

- Insurance Policy: A contract (generally a standard form contract) between the insurer and the insured, known as the policyholder, which determines the claims the insurer is legally required to pay in exchange for an initial payment, known as the premium.

- In-Network Provider: A healthcare provider (such as physician or hospital) that is contracted with your health insurance company to be part of its network of healthcare providers and to accept contracted (reduced) reimbursement rates.

- Managed Care: Describes a variety of techniques intended to reduce the cost of providing health benefits and improve the quality of care. Managed care services are generally provided by a contracted network of healthcare professionals.

- Medicare: A national social insurance program that guarantees access to health insurance for Americans aged 65 and older, as well as younger people with disabilities, end stage renal disease, or Amyotrophic lateral sclerosis.

- Medicaid: A government health program for persons of all ages whose income and resources are insufficient to pay for health care.

- Obamacare (See Patient Protection and Affordable Care Act): The unofficial name for the Patient Protection and Affordable Care Act (See "The Affordable Care Act").

- Out-of-Network Provider: A provider that isn't contracted with your health insurance company and won't accept its contracted rates as reimbursement.

- The Patient Protection and Affordable Care Act (See Obamacare): The Patient Protection and Affordable Care Act was signed into law by President Obama in 2010. It is focused on health care funding, reducing the cost of healthcare for everyone, increasing coverage, and removing obstacles to healthcare.

- Point of Service Plan (POS): A type of managed care health insurance system that combines characteristics of both HMO and PPO.

- Preferred Provider Organization (PPO): A managed care organization of medical doctors, hospitals and other healthcare providers who have covenanted with an insurer to provide health care at reduced rates to the insurer's or clients.

- <u>Premiums</u>: Payments you make to your health insurance company to continue your health insurance policy.

- <u>Premium Tax Credits</u>: Subsidies provided by Obamacare that allows tax credits for low-income families to purchase private health insurance through the health insurance exchanges.

- <u>Pre-Existing Conditions</u>: Medical conditions that have occurred prior to applying for health insurance coverage.

- <u>Preventive Services</u>: Medical and other services designed to keep you healthy. Also known as "wellness" services.

- <u>Prior Authorization</u>: A requirement to seek approval or permission from your health insurance company before you receive certain high-cost medical services.

- <u>Retail Medical Clinics</u>: Walk-in clinics located in retail stores, supermarkets and pharmacies that treat uncomplicated, minor illnesses and provide preventive healthcare services.

- <u>Retirement Account Hardship Distribution</u>: Money distributed or withdrawn from a retirement account without penalties to pay for medical services. This "last resort" option is reserved only for certain limited circumstances, such as for unreimbursed medical expenses that are more than 7.5% of adjusted gross income.

- Surgery Center: A free-standing medical facility that performs outpatient surgeries, pain management services, and certain diagnostic procedures not requiring an overnight stay in the hospital.

- Urgent Care Centers: Walk-in clinics focused on the delivery of ambulatory care in a dedicated medical facility outside of a traditional emergency room. Urgent care centers primarily treat injuries or illnesses requiring immediate care, but not serious enough to require an ER visit.

<<>>

Index

Advanced Breast Cancer Community, 60
Advocacy for Patients with Chronic Illness, 63
Affiliation Period, 33
Affordable Care Act, 115, 156
Alliance of Claims Assistance Professionals, 128
American Association of Diabetes Educators, 61
American Breast Cancer Foundation, 60
American Cancer Society, 60
American College of Cardiology, 61
American Diabetes Association, 61
American Heart Association, 61
American Stroke Association, 62
Annual Benefits, 79, 80
Appeal, 35, 124, 125
Association Cancer On-line Resources, 60
Avon Foundation, 60
Benefits, 41, 42, 71, 114, 147, 149, 153
Billadvocate.com, 128
Billing Errors, 120
Brand-Name Medications (Drugs), 26, 67, 107, 109, 110, 115, 141, 152
BreastCancer.org, 60
California Department of Corporations, 35
California Department of Health Services, 35
California Department of Insurance, 35
California Department of Managed Healthcare, 35
Cancer Financial Assistance Coalition, 60
Cancer Support Community, 60
CancerCare, 60
Care Harbor, 59
Catastrophic Health Insurance Plan, 29, 149
Chapman Consulting Group, 128
Charles Ray III Diabetes Association, Inc., 61
Children's Health Insurance Program, 72, 146
Cleveland Clinic Heart Center, 61
ClinicalTrials.gov, 62
COBRA, 31, 53, 54, 55, 56, 57, 58, 150

Co-insurance, 20, 27, 30, 43, 44, 48, 50, 66, 68, 72, 79, 80, 105
Concierge Medicine, 94, 151
Copayment, 43, 151
Cosmetic surgery, 31, 66
Costco, 111, 146
Coverage, 36, 41, 74, 76, 83, 108, 151
CVS Pharmacy, 100, 111, 146
Deductible, 24, 25, 26, 27, 28, 29, 31, 43, 44, 45, 46, 47, 48, 49, 51, 65, 74, 79, 80, 81, 82, 83, 89, 101, 120, 134, 140, 151, 153, 154
Diabeteslocal.org, 61
Emergency Room, 100
Employer waiting period, 33
Evidence of Coverage, 76, 77, 78, 151
Explanation of Benefits (EOB), 119, 120, 121, 122, 125, 129, 152
Fairhealthconsumer.org, 91
Fee-For-Service (FFS), 23, 24, 25, 27, 29, 30, 34, 39, 40, 41, 69, 152
Flexible Spending Account, 133, 134, 153
GoodRx (Pharmacy App), 112
Group Healthcare Insurance, 22
Health and Human Services, 37, 60, 143, 144

Health Insurance, 17, 19, 21, 22, 33, 35, 36, 37, 45, 50, 54, 55, 63, 72, 73, 75, 77, 89, 92, 99, 108, 150, 151, 152, 153, 154, 155, 156, 157, 158
Health Maintenance Organization (HMO), 25, 26, 27, 30, 34, 35, 66, 87, 153, 156
Health Savings Account, 134
Healthcare Benefits, 21, 22, 33, 54, 57, 76
Healthcarebluebook.com, 91, 128, 146, 147
HealthWell Foundation, 60
Heart Rhythm Society, 62
High Deductible Health Plan, 28, 154
Hospital Acquired Condition, 121
Income Tax Deduction, 135, 154
Individual Health Insurance, 23, 56, 154
In-Network (Healthcare Providers), 17, 34, 77, 79, 92, 93, 151
Insurance Policy, 30, 154
Internet Stroke Center, 62
IRS, 131, 135, 136, 137, 147, 155
ISNET, 128, 147
Kmart, 111, 146
Lifehappens.org, 91
Limited Visit Benefits, 81
LowestMed (Pharmacy App), 112

Managed Care, 25, 29, 39, 40, 65, 77, 153, 155, 156, 157
Mandatory coverage, 36
Medicaid, 5, 18, 33, 37, 50, 68, 70, 71, 72, 73, 74, 87, 143, 145
Medical Bill, 119, 122, 126, 152, 157
Medical Board of California, 35
Medical Cost Advocates, 128, 147
Medicare, 5, 18, 33, 37, 50, 56, 64, 65, 66, 67, 68, 69, 70, 71, 72, 73, 74, 87, 90, 108, 115, 143, 145
Medicine Program, 114, 147
Mended Hearts, Inc., 61
National Association of Free Clinics, 59, 144
National Cancer Institute, 60
National Diabetes Information Clearinghouse, 61
National Institutes of Health, 62
National Organization of Rare Disorders, 62
National Stroke Association, 62
Needymeds, 114, 146
Never Events, 121
NewChoiceHealth, Inc., 128
Obama, Barack President of the United States of America, 35
Obamacare, 3, 5, 17, 18, 30, 35, 36, 37, 41, 44, 49, 50, 51, 67, 73, 108, 115, 116, 131, 132, 137, 143, 156, 158
OTC Plus (Pharmacy App), 112
Out-of-Network (Healthcare Provider), 24, 28, 30, 34, 92, 93, 123, 126
Part A Hospital, 65, 67, 68, 74
Part B Medical, 65, 66, 68, 70, 74
Part C Medicare Advantage, 66, 74
Part D Medicare Prescription Drugs, 66, 67, 68, 74, 115
Partnership for Prescription Assistance, 113, 146
Patient Access Network Foundation, 63
Patient Advocacy Foundation, 62
Patient Advocate Foundation, 128
Patient Assistance Program Center, 113, 114, 146
Patient Protection and Affordable Care Act, 3, 35, 156
Pharmaceutical Company Rebates, Trial Offers, Discount Cards, 113

Pharmacycard, 114, 146
Planned Parenthood, 59
Point of Service (POS), 25, 26, 27, 28, 30, 156
Pre-Existing Conditions, 20, 31, 34, 36, 37, 54, 56, 58
Preferred Provider Organization (PPO), 25, 26, 27, 28, 29, 32, 35, 66, 87, 156, 157
Premiums, 19, 20, 21, 22, 23, 24, 28, 30, 31, 43, 44, 45, 46, 47, 48, 50, 51, 55, 57, 58, 65, 66, 67, 68, 72, 74, 132, 137, 140, 149, 150, 153, 154
Prescription Drugs, 18, 19, 26, 29, 41, 43, 65, 66, 67, 82, 101, 107, 108, 110, 112, 113, 115, 116, 133
Prescription Saver (Pharmacy App), 112
Prior Authorization, 77, 78, 79
Private Insurance, 18, 21, 23, 69, 72, 132
Prostate Cancer Foundation, 61
Prostate Cancer Info Link, 61
Prostate Conditions Education Council, 61
Retail Medical Clinic, 98
Retirement Account Hardship Distribution, 136
Rising Medical Services, 128, 147
RTH Foundation, 62
Rx Outreach, 111, 146
RxHope, 114, 147
Smart Medical Consumer, 128
Social Security, 65, 68, 71, 72, 145, 158
State Medical Assistance, 68, 70, 145
Stroke Network, 62
Supplemental Security Income, 72
Surgery Center (Outpatient), 102, 158
Survivorship A-Z, 63
Susan G. Komen Foundation, 60
Target, 100, 111, 146
Tax Credits, 51, 131, 132, 137, 158
Urgent Care Center, 100, 101, 158
Xubex, 114
Zero: The Project to End Prostate Cancer, 61

<<>>

Notes

Made in the USA
San Bernardino, CA
31 August 2018